SPIRITUALITY
AND PASTORAL CARE

Jan. 1988

THE AUTHOR

Kenneth Leech is a graduate of King's College,
London and Trinity College, Oxford. He trained for
the priesthood at St Stephen's House, Oxford and
was ordained in 1964. He worked for several years in
the East End of London and in Soho among drug
addicts, and wrote *A Practical Guide to the Drug Scene*,
which has been acclaimed as the best book written
on the problems of drug dependence. He is also the
author of *Youthquake*, a study of the 1950s and 1960s,
Soul Friend, a study of Christian spirituality, and its
successors *True Prayer* and *True God*. He has written
for many journals, and broadcasts frequently on
television and radio. From 1971–74 he was chaplain
of St Augustine's College, Canterbury, and from
1974–80 he was Rector of St Matthew's, Bethnal
Green. He is presently Race Relations Field Officer
for the Board for Social Responsibility.

Kenneth Leech

SPIRITUALITY AND PASTORAL CARE

SHELDON PRESS
LONDON

First published in Great Britain in 1986 by
Sheldon Press, SPCK, Marylebone Road, London NW1 4DU

British Library Cataloguing in Publication Data

Leech, Kenneth, *1939*–
    Spirituality and pastoral care.
    1. Spirituality
    I. Title
    248.4   BV501.2

    ISBN 0-85969-520-4

Photoset and printed in Great Britain by
WBC Print Ltd, Bristol

Contents

Preface   1

PART I
Foundations of Spirituality

1   Spirituality and the Word of God   5
2   Spirituality and Silence   17
3   Spirituality and Struggle   31

PART II
Spiritual Direction

4   Spiritual Direction and the Contemporary
      Climate   47
5   Direction, Counselling and Psychotherapy   55
6   The Prophetic Dimension in Spiritual Direction   66
7   Spiritual Direction and the Practice of Ministry   75

PART III
Spirituality in Practice: A Study of Four Pastors

8   Brother Neville: Contemplative Among the
      Poor   85
9   Stanley Evans: The Kingdom of God in the
      Back Streets   95
10 Hugh Maycock: Astonished at the Divine
      Beauty   105
11 Colin Winter: The Breaking Process   115

12 Spirituality and the Renewal of the Priesthood   127

Notes   137
Acknowledgements   145
Index   147

Preface

The chapters in this book, apart from the last, were originally given as lectures at different times and in different places. The first three chapters were given as the Hopkins Lectures at the First Methodist Church, Denton, Texas, in February 1984. I am grateful to the Hopkins family and to the Revd Dr William Crouch for the invitation to inaugurate this series of lectures. Chapters 4-7 were given in the University of Chicago in 1982, and were originally sponsored by the Catholic Theological Union and St Stephen's House. They were later given at Nashotah House, Wisconsin. Chapters 8-11 are based upon a retreat for those being ordained in the Diocese of Birmingham at Petertide 1983.

Together these chapters are concerned with the central theme of the relationship of spirituality and ministry. They move from a consideration of the foundations of spirituality through a discussion of the growing ministry of spiritual direction, and end with reflections on spirituality in practice based upon the lives and witness of four priests. I hope that they may do something to overcome the gap between spiritual life and pastoral practice.

Part I
Foundations of Spirituality

1
Spirituality and the Word of God

Christian spirituality is about a process of formation, a process in which we are formed by, and in, Christ: Christ who, sharing the form of God, assumed the form of a servant (Phil. 2.6). In this process, we are *transformed* so that we come more and more to share the Christ nature. Spiritual formation, then, is not a process of self-cultivation by which we are helped to adjust, to *conform* to the values of the dominant social order. Spiritual formation is not about adjustment. It is a process of 'Christ-ening', of being clothed with Christ, and in this process we are transformed. It is a process which involves confrontation, exploration and struggle, and its goal is maturity in Christ. Let me emphasize these three elements.

First, Christian spirituality is a process in which Christ takes the initiative. It is a putting on of Christ (Gal. 3.27), a solidarity in Christ, a sharing in his dying and rising. It is a process which the Incarnation began, and which continues, a process which the Orthodox theologian Paul Evdokimov calls 'Christification'.[1] It is therefore a work of grace from start to finish.

Secondly, in this process there is confrontation, exploration and struggle. In these first three chapters, I shall look specifically at confrontation by the Word of God in Scripture; exploration of the depths of our being through the practice of silence and solitude; and struggle, both interior, as we encounter darkness and inner turmoil, and exterior, as we wrestle with structures which are inimical to spiritual growth. Spiritual formation therefore is not a gentle path, the acquisition and application of spiritual skills and techniques. It is a road which passes through storms and desert wastes, through fire and flood; a road traversed by monsters and demons; a road fraught with danger.

Thirdly, the goal of our spirituality is Christian maturity. This is not the same as psychological maturity, adjustment, the attainment of a balanced personality. It is a theological goal which will bring us into collision with prevailing values, and will therefore bring threats to our adjustment and our peace of mind. It will also bring us into collision with much that passes for Christianity and for spirituality in our society.

In this process of spirituality, the Bible has a central place. But if we are to begin a movement 'back to the Bible', we must recognize the formidable obstacles in our path. Seventy years ago the Christian socialist priest Charles Marson wrote a profound and hilariously funny polemic on the misuse of the Bible in schools. Entitled *Huppim and Muppim and Ard* – the three sons of Benjamin in Genesis 46.21 – it attacked forms of 'religious education' which focused on the minutiae of Scripture while utterly missing the point of its teaching. He wrote:[2]

These children can tell you who Huppim and Muppim and Ard were; they know the latitude of Beersheba, Kerioth and Beth-gamal; they can tell you who slew a lion in a pit on a snowy day; they have ripe views upon the identity of Nathanael and St Bartholomew; they can name the destructive miracles, the parables peculiar to St Luke, and, above all, they have a masterly knowledge of St Paul's second missionary journey. They are well loaded and ballasted with chronicles of Baasha and Zimri, Methuselah and Alexander the Coppersmith . . . Therefore while our clergy are . . . instant in season and out of season . . . to proclaim the glories of Huppim and

Muppim, the people are destroyed for lack of knowledge
. . . They know all about Abraham except the way to his
bosom, all about David except his sure mercies, and all
about St Paul except the faith which he preached and
which justified him.

Those days are not passed. The misuse of Scripture takes
many forms. We see a meticulous study of the text
combined with an utter incapacity to be challenged by the
Word. We see a fanatical adherence to the words of
Scripture combined with a terrifying degree of intolerance
and hatred. In many parts of the United States, crude
fundamentalism has grown to the level of a serious illness;
in James Barr's words, 'a pathological condition of
Christianity'.[3] So a willingness to be formed by the Word
must begin with a painful and penitent recognition of the
ways in which the Bible has been misused to reinforce
oppression, violence, injustice, and the powerful interests
of dominant social classes and groups.

Fundamentalism of this aggressive, crusading type is
essentially hostile to spiritual progress for at least three
reasons. First, it is unintelligent. The relationship between
Scripture and the disciple is seen as that of master to slave.
It does not allow for that honest struggle of mind and heart
by which truth is revealed. William Sloane Coffin, minister
at Riverside Church, New York, once compared the Bible
to a mirror. 'If an ass peers in, you can't expect an apostle
to peer out.' Secondly, it is the religion of a crusading
mind rather than of a crucified mind. True spirituality
involves a dimension of listening, of abandonment, of silent
brooding, features which are conspicuously absent in most
fundamentalist worship and life. For the crusading mind,
the Bible becomes a weapon. Thirdly, it is selective. It
chooses those parts of Scripture which fit in with the
dominant ideology. So, for example, it often focuses more
on issues such as homosexuality and abortion, on which the

7

Bible says little or nothing, and ignores issues such as poverty and wealth, on which it says a great deal. Being itself so entangled with the dominant ideology, it fails to see how conditioned and unfree – and therefore anti-spiritual – its biblicism is.

If we are to be formed by the Word, we need to cultivate the opposite qualities: insight, contemplative listening, and the willingness to allow our culture not to distort the Word but to be confronted and challenged by it. If the Bible is to play an important part in our spirituality, we need to begin with the realization that much of our contemporary spirituality is not sufficiently biblical, indeed often not biblical at all.

For example, much current spirituality has been moulded to suit a narcissistic culture. It is a spirituality of self-cultivation, of personal enlightenment, of heightened awareness. It is often more akin to classical gnosticism, with its concern for self-knowledge and illumination, than to the biblical tradition, with its stress on the salvation and sanctification of a people. Much of this spirituality is gnostic also in its commitment to a dualism of spirit and matter, and its failure to understand the incarnational basis of Christian spiritual formation. By its false division of reality into spiritual and material, it creates a religion in which true spirituality comes to be concerned simply with 'the condition of the inward soul of man' and with 'the ethereal qualities of immortality'.[4] Such a concern is then contrasted with concerns for social justice, for the transforming of structures, for global peace and reconciliation. Such a division is alien to true spirituality as understood in the biblical tradition. Again, much current spirituality seems less concerned with the transformation of our lives in and through the incarnate Word than with the provision of comfort, reassurance and inner peace. In Jim Wallis's words, Jesus is seen not as changing our lives but improving them. 'Modern conversion brings Jesus into our lives rather than bringing us into his.'[5] So it is that much contemporary spiritual striving has lost its roots in biblical Christianity. Let me now suggest a number of ways in which a biblical perspective on spiritual formation will help to correct much that is false in current approaches.

First, biblical spirituality is social spirituality. It is a spirituality of the Kingdom of God, of a pilgrim people, of the Body of Christ. The image of the *soma Christou*, the Body of Christ, is central to the New Testament teaching on spiritual growth. In his influential study *The Body*,[6] the late John Robinson described it as the keystone of Pauline theology. The language of spiritual formation in St Paul's letters is social language. He speaks of mutual encouragement in faith (Rom. 1.12) and of mutual upbuilding (14.19); of our being 'one body in Christ' (Rom. 12.5; 1 Cor. 10.17;12.12). The manifestations of the Spirit are given for the 'common good' (1 Cor. 12.7), for building up the church, the Body of Christ (1 Cor. 14.12; Eph. 4.12). He speaks of a solidarity in holiness: if the first fruits are holy, so is the whole; if the root is holy, so are the branches (Rom. 11.16). To move from the intensely individualistic religion of our day to St Paul's letters is to enter an entirely different realm. There is in fact very little in the New Testament letters about personal spiritual formation as such. The centre of gravity is always the body, the solidarity; its spirituality is social. To be a Christian, to be *en Christo*, is to be part of an organism, a new community, the extension of the Incarnation.

Secondly, in the New Testament we find a view of spirituality as progress towards maturity. The stress is not on inner peace and adjustment, but rather on movement and pilgrimage. In the language of the Texan priest Wes Seeliger, it is a spirituality for pioneers rather than settlers.[7] Let me take these two themes of progress and of maturity in Christ, looking primarily at the teaching of the New Testament letters.

9

For Paul, our hope is that we may come to share the glory of God (Rom. 5.2). We begin as babes in Christ (1 Cor. 3.1). But God gives growth (3.7). Again, as with the teaching as a whole, the language of growth is primarily social language. It is the structure, the Christian community, which grows, and we are built into it (Eph. 2.21–2). This growth includes the movement towards a fuller understanding of the mysteries of faith. Now we see in a glass darkly, but we will see face to face (1 Cor. 13.9,12). It is a movement also which takes place in Christ, a movement in which we are being changed into Christ's likeness, from one degree of glory to another (2 Cor. 3.18), a theme picked up in one of the earliest eucharistic hymns. It is an interior process, for our inner nature is being renewed daily (2 Cor. 4.16). It is a process which is not without pain for the pastors. Paul described himself as being 'in travail until Christ be formed in you' (Gal. 4.19). In Philippians, the language of pressing on (3.12) and straining forward (3.13) is used. However, the initiative in this process of spiritual growth and formation is Christ's. This is made very clear in Colossians. 'You have come to fulness of life in him' (2.10). Yet although the process has already been initiated, there is still growth for the whole body 'grows with a growth that is from God' (2.19). There is both a past event and a present abiding: we have died, and our lives are hidden with Christ in God (3.3). Christ is the beginning of the process and its goal. To be a Christian then is not simply to believe in Christ or to imitate Christ, but to be formed by, and moulded by, Christ.

In the spiritual progress of which the New Testament speaks, there is a stress on the centrality of love as opposed to knowledge or mental enlightenment. Knowledge, *gnōsis*, puffs up, while love builds up (1 Cor. 8.1). Love is really basic, and without it even the prophetic gifts are useless (13.2ff). There are one or two references to 'training', in godliness (1 Tim. 4.7) or in righteousness (2 Tim. 3.17). In

Ephesians, we find a reference to inner strengthening, and this is linked with being filled with the fulness of God (Eph. 3.16). There is a reference also to enlightening the eyes of the heart (1.18), an image which appears later in mystical writers.

The progress of which the letters speak is spiritual progress. Christians, all Christians, are called to be *pneumatikoi*, spiritual persons (1 Cor. 2.13f). In 1 Cor. 15 the body of the resurrection is called a *sōma pneumatikon* (15.44ff). To be spiritual at all is to share in Christ's risen life, to be formed anew in him. Spirituality is inseparable from this solidarity in Christ. When Paul speaks of spiritual discernment (1 Cor. 2.14), he links it with sharing the mind of Christ (2.16). But it is not possible to share Christ's mind without sharing in Christ's body. Again, it is by the Spirit that we are able to pray 'Abba' as Christ himself does (Rom. 8.15–16; Gal. 4.6). But this too is inseparable from the social and even cosmic liberation of which Paul goes on to speak (Rom. 8.21ff).

Spiritual formation then, according to the New Testament letters, is a way of progress in which we are formed in, and grow in, Christ; and its goal is maturity, perfection.

The word translated 'mature', *teleios*, is used in the Pauline letters in close association with the theme of progress. Maturity does not come quickly, though Paul points out that there are some who wrongly see themselves as *teleioi* (Col. 2.6; Phil. 3.15). 'The mature', he claims, are those who are able to receive the wisdom of God, 'those who are ripe for it' (1 Cor. 2.6 NEB). He urges the Corinthians to be mature in their thinking (14.20). In Ephesians he speaks of the mature humanity which is identified with 'the stature of the fulness of Christ' (4.13) and with the growth of the body in love (4.16). In Philippians, maturity is connected with 'straining forward' (3.13–15). Paul insists that he himself has not yet reached maturity (Phil. 3–12), but he goes on to speak of 'those of us

11

who are mature' (3.15). Maturity is certainly something to be prayed for (Col. 4.12). In Hebrews, Jesus is said to have become *teleios* through suffering (1.10). Later in the letter, the author tells his readers that 'solid food is for the mature' (5.14), and they are defined as those who have been trained to distinguish good from evil. The writer urges his readers to 'go on to maturity' (6.1).

Maturity then is to do with sharing the mind of Christ. Paul speaks of being not conformed but rather transformed (Rom. 12.2). The spirituality which we seek must be a spirituality of nonconformity and of transformation. Such a maturity in Christ will seem like folly to most people, for it is necessary to become a fool in order to become truly wise (1 Cor. 3.18). Perfection and folly are closely linked in Christian spirituality as John Saward's magnificent study *Perfect Fools* shows.[8] We should not therefore confuse Christian maturity with social conformity or adjustment to convention. 'I cannot escape the feeling,' writes Richard Lovelace,[9] 'that Luther, Bunyan and the Apostle Paul would be referred to psychotherapists if they appeared in the evangelical community today.' Martin Luther King, preaching on the text 'Be not conformed' (Rom. 12.2), spoke of the need for Christians to be both nonconformist and 'creativity maladjusted' *vis-à-vis* the world.[10]

Christian maturity, spiritual formation, is identified by the New Testament letters as putting on a new nature (Eph. 4.23), putting on the Lord Jesus Christ (Rom. 13.14). We have already put on Christ in the sacrament of baptism (Gal. 3.27). We are in Christ, and because of this a new creation is in being (2 Cor. 5.17). Christ lives in us (Gal. 2.20; 6.15). Paul also teaches that Christ is in the form of God (Phil. 2.6) and that we are to become like him (3.10). We are to 'live in him, rooted and built up in him' (Col. 2.6–7). The nature which we share is daily 'being renewed . . . after the image of its Creator' (Col. 3.10). Although the idea of the 'imitation of Christ' is implicit in 1

Cor. 11.1 (and in Eph. 5.1 and 1 Thess. 1.6), this is not the dominant idea in the New Testament. Rather we are being urged to live in Christ, in whom we are already incorporate, and whose nature we share.

To sum up, the New Testament letters offer us three major insights into Christian spiritual formation: it is a social act, rooted in the Christian community, the Body of Christ; it is a process involving growth and progress towards maturity; and it is a putting on and sharing of Christ's nature.

The Scriptures teach us the importance of spiritual growth. But how can we use those Scriptures as a means to spiritual growth, as an instrument of transformation? How can we be formed by the Word? In the New Testament, the Word of God is seen as an integral element in the process of spiritual formation. We have been born anew through the Word (1 Pet. 1.23). It is near us, on our lips and in our hearts (Rom. 10.8). We are urged to live according to Scripture (1 Cor. 4.6). The Word is to dwell in us richly (Col. 3.16). We are to hold firm to it (Titus 1.9), to be 'doers of the Word' not only hearers (Jas. 1.22). The Word is seen as powerful, divisive, purgative, and discerning. So in Hebrews 4.12 we read:

> The Word of God is living and active, sharper than any two-edged sword, piercing to the division of soul and spirit, of joints and marrow, and discerning the thoughts and intentions of the heart.

The writer goes on to say that all is 'laid bare' by the Word, and later speaks of tasting the Word (6.5).

If we are to be faithful to this understanding of the Word and its role in our movement towards maturity, we need to take seriously such themes as the power of the Word, the intimacy of the Word (as brought out in the language of touch and taste) and the Word as an instrument of spiritual discernment. I will therefore suggest three approaches to the use of Scripture in spiritual formation, and I will call them wrestling, brooding, and weeding. (Though I would advise people not to mix the metaphors!)

First, wrestling. I take the image from the story of Jacob wrestling with God (Gen. 32.24–32). Two features of the story are worth noting. First, at the end of the exhausting encounter, Jacob emerges still not knowing the name of God (32.29). There remains the sense of mystery and incompleteness. Secondly, he emerges wounded (32.25, 32). Spiritual maturity does not imply the absence of wounds. Indeed, the ascent to truth may only be possible at the risk of brokenness. In the encounter between the Word of God and the dilemmas and perplexities of our day, there is no straightforward question/answer process. We simply cannot proceed direct from the Year of Jubilee in Leviticus 25 to the problems of international debt and land tenure; or from the apostolic *koinōnia* of the early chapters of Acts (with the awful consequences for Ananias and Sapphira who violated it) to the current debates about redistribution of wealth and capital punishment. The link is not that simple. It involves allowing the truth of Scripture to enter into dialogue, struggle and conflict with the contemporary reality. Insight comes not by direct application but through and in the conflict. In order for this to happen there needs to be a twofold process: grappling with the Word of God, and grappling with the issues in our world, in our neighbourhood, in our personal lives. It is a central task of the church, nationally and locally, to seek to interpret the Word of God in relation to the conflicts of our day. The Vatican 2 document *Gaudium at Spes* expresses it thus:[11]

> With the help of the Holy Spirit, it is the task of the entire People of God, especially pastors and theologians, to hear,

distinguish and interpret the many voices of our age, and to judge them in the light of the divine Word. In this way revealed truth can always be more deeply penetrated, better understood, and set forth to greater advantage.

A local church which seeks to guide its members in a responsible spirituality needs to encourage this wrestling process, a process by which together we struggle with the Word of God and the voices of our day, seeking to grow in understanding and response through the encounter.

Secondly, brooding. The Greek word *meletē*, from which we derive our word 'meditation', meant ceaseless brooding. In its origins in early Egyptian monasticism, meditation meant a prayerful repetition of biblical texts. Pachomius's monks learned Scripture by heart. Today far too much of the biblical study is academic in a negative sense. If we are to recover a central place for Scripture in the life of the Spirit, we need to develop a contemplative approach; and this involves digesting the Word inwardly. Brooding on the Scriptures is necessary if we are to acquire a biblical consciousness, a biblical spirituality, and this has important consequences for the use of Scripture liturgically, in the daily Office, and in the Eucharist.

To use the Bible in a contemplative way is to experience something of what the letter to the Hebrews means by 'tasting the Word of God' (6.5). Again, a main task of the local church is to encourage such prayerful brooding; to make provision for it; and to guide people in its practice.

Thirdly, weeding. It is important to approach Scripture with what the South American theologian Juan Luis Segundo calls ideological and exegetical suspicion: that is, with the assumption that the meaning of Scripture has been coloured and distorted by the dominant culture.[12] It is necessary therefore to allow the Word to cut through the distorted interpretations, and this is not an easy process because we are all creatures of our time and of our society.

15

Hence the subversive character of the work of discernment, for it calls into question all our partial perceptions, exposing them to the scrutiny of the Word of God. It is essential to disentangle the message of the Gospel from the accumulation of cultural baggage with which it has been covered. This calls for a process of purification, involving prayer, critical reflection, and corporate debate. It is a central task of the local church to promote questioning and the spirit of weeding. Only in this way can we be enabled to discover and taste the hidden fruit.

In these three images of the wrestler, the reflective brooder, and the weeder, there is a common element: ruthless persistence. There is struggle till the break of day; there is uninterrupted, contemplative reflection in solitude; and there is tireless removal of weeds and obstacles. In our encounter with the Word of God, we will need to maintain such a threefold pattern, and a local church should be helping to provide:

a wrestling centre, a forum in which there can be open debate and struggle on the crises of the day in the light of biblical insights;

a still point where individuals can find the space and the solitude for the necessary inner creative brooding and prayerful reading;

facilities for continual weeding, purging, clarifying, of the truths of the Gospel message.

Only in this way can Scripture come to live in us, to unsettle us, to grow within us, to unify our vision. The aim of this process is that we become a biblical people: a people formed and nourished by the Word, a people of contradiction and of authentic nonconformity.

2
Spirituality and Silence

During one of the episodes of 'The Goon Show', one of Britain's most memorable comedy shows, the telephone rang. 'Who is speaking?', the answering goon enquired. 'Who is that? Who is that speaking? Who is it? Who is there? Who is speaking?' After a pause, a voice said, '*You* are speaking.' It could be a perfect description of much of our prayer life: we are speaking. More generally, it could also be a description of much of the current interest in 'spirituality'. Undoubtedly, spirituality is in again. There is a lot of it about. But there is a very great danger that the current vogue of interest will turn spirituality into yet another subject for talk and discussion. We speak about it. We run courses in it. We award diplomas for it. We write books, give lectures, record cassettes and videos about it. And yet this accumulation of material may contribute to the process of spiritual formation – precisely nothing. Spirituality is being offered as an interesting area, a diversion, and, as such, can provide yet another protection from the living God. For without doubt spirituality can be a way of escaping from God by erecting a religious zone between God and ourselves.

In the previous chapter it was suggested that much contemporary spirituality is non-biblical, and that it is important to read the Scriptures in an attitude of silence and struggle. Struggle: so that the Word of contradiction, the Word which is sharper than a two-edged sword, may cut through the illusion, the falsehood, the idolatry of our culture and ourselves. Silence: so that we may taste the

Word, digest it, absorb it until it becomes part of our being and transforms us.

If this encounter with the Word of God in silence is to occur, we need nothing less than a revolution in our social, cultural and religious structures which are so organized as to prevent silence from playing more than an accidental part of our lives. This hostility to silence represents a serious break with the Christian spiritual tradition which, from the earliest times, saw silence and solitude as essential constitutive elements in a developing life of prayer and progress towards Christian maturity. It saw silence and solitude as the points at which the ministry of attentiveness, of listening to the skies, and discerning the signs, could take place.

One of the earliest testimonies to the place of silence in the Christian life comes in the writings of Ignatius of Antioch, a contemporary of the New Testament. It is better to keep quiet and be, says Ignatius, than to be fluent and not be. He speaks of the silences of Jesus, and links the attainment of silence with 'full spiritual maturity' (Eph. 15). He claims that the three major events in the work of salvation – the virginity of Mary, the Incarnation, and the death of Christ – were brought to pass in 'the deep silence of God', that is, in the depths of God's being (Eph. 19). Christ himself is described as the Word who proceeds from silence (Magn. 8). Thus anyone who would enter into the depths of God's mysterious activity and of his very being must begin to practise a theology of silence. This is, of course, in line with the refusal of the biblical tradition to name God or to define him. The God of Israel is a God who is known in his works, and known in the darkness and silence of Sinai and Calvary, known as a hidden God. The apophatic or negative theology of the eastern church, in which God is spoken of only in negation, testifies to the incapacity of words and concepts to penetrate the reality of God. Talking about God is in fact one of the things which the Bible hardly permits us to do. It is in silence, in awe and amazement, that the disciple comes to understand the mystery of God. It is in silence that we come closest to the reality of prayer as attention and waiting. In the words of the nineteenth-century Russian Theophan the Recluse: 'The principal thing is to stand before God with the mind in the heart, and to go on standing before him unceasingly day and night until the end of time.'[1]

Thus from the earliest times silence has been emphasized by the experienced guides in the spiritual life. The Sayings of the Desert Fathers of the fourth and fifth centuries are filled with admonitions on the value of silence. 'God is silence' said the fifth-century Syrian monk John the Solitary. The attainment of *hesychia*, inner silence, became the central feature of the orthodox spiritual movement which centred on Mount Athos, and whose principal devotional manifestation was the Jesus Prayer. *Hesychia* meant more than the absence of noise. It denoted the condition of inner vigilance and attention, of waiting upon God, of uninterrupted prayerfulness, the prayer of the heart. It is interesting, and highly significant, that the two post-biblical saints who are honoured by the title 'theologian' in the eastern church, St Gregory Nazianzus and St Symeon, both stress the place of silence and interior peace among the qualities of the theologian. One of the essential marks of the theologian, says Gregory, is inner calm – so as not like madmen to lose our breath'.[2] He saw how fatal such breathlessness was to spiritual sanity. Yet at times one feels that breathlessness is the fundamental feature of much church life.

The centrality of silence is stressed also in medieval Western mystical writers. 'In silence and quietness,' writes Thomas à Kempis, 'the devout soul makes progress and learns the hidden mysteries of the Scriptures'.[3] Silence is seen as a vital element in spirituality by writers as diverse as the Carmelite St John of the Cross and the Quaker George

Fox. In the twentieth century no writer has done more to emphasize the dimension of silence in Christian life than the late Thomas Merton. In his poem 'The Quickening of St John the Baptist', Merton expresses something of the ministry of watching, of silent attention.

> Night is our diocese, and silence is our ministry.
> Poverty our charity, and helplessness our tongue-tied
>   sermon.
> Beyond the scope of sight or sound we dwell upon the
>   air,
> Seeking the world's gain in an unthinkable experience.
> We are exiles in the far end of solitude, living as
>   listeners,
> With hearts attending to the skies we cannot
>   understand,
> Waiting upon the first far drums of Christ the
>   Conqueror,
> Planted like sentinels upon the world's frontier.[4]

Merton is, of course, thinking of the role of the contemplative. But one can apply what he says in some sense to all Christian people in whom the dimension of 'discerning the signs of the times' needs to find a place.

Is the tradition correct in the importance it places upon silence? I believe it is, and that the neglect of silence in our spiritual life today is a deficiency of alarmingly serious dimensions. Why are silence and solitude so important?

First, silence and solitude are valuable paths to self-knowledge which is the first necessary step in the knowledge of God. If we are truly to know ourselves, to accept ourselves, without fear of the darkness and the turmoil within us, we need to cultivate the gift of silence. In silence and solitude, we can enter into ourselves, moving beyond the frenzy of endless activity, whether of body or of mind, which can stand in the way of any real encounter with our true selves.

Secondly, silence and solitude are ways of deepening the life of contemplative prayer, allowing the Holy Spirit to enter into and pray deeply within us. Indeed silence and solitude are the necessary conditions of contemplation. Moving beyond words and concepts, we wait upon God in the emptiness and nothingness of what the mystics call 'unknowing'. Prayer becomes very simple, almost wordless, loving attention. In this way the Holy Spirit can take over our prayer so that it becomes more and more the Spirit praying within us.

John Main

Thirdly, silence and solitude are important elements in pastoral practice. Nothing is more necessary in pastoral care and in spiritual direction than the ability to listen, an ability which is nourished in contemplation, stillness and inner silence. More than any other pastoral gifts, people are looking for pastors who are possessed of interior quietude. It is not a skill that can be learnt, nor can one fake such a quality. It only comes as a by-product of a life in which silence and stillness have a major place.

In the Christian tradition, there are two symbols which recur frequently in the literature of contemplative prayer: the symbols of Desert and of Dark Night. The Desert symbol spans the spiritual history of the people of God from Abraham's movement into unknown territory, through the wanderings in the wilderness, the desert movement of the early church, to Charles de Foucauld and the revival of desert spirituality in the twentieth century. It stands for the realities of purity, of simplicity, of conflict, and of revelation. The Dark Night, a term popularized by St John of the Cross, takes up the symbolism of darkness from the eastern tradition of negative theology. It stands for the life of faith, and specifically for the point in the journey when words and concepts have run their course, and one enters a dark night. Together the symbols of Desert and Dark Night accurately represent the spiritual path beyond the limitations of language, a path calling us to a radical

21

purification and to an encounter with darkness. How then can the symbols of Desert and Dark Night speak to our spiritual needs?

First, the Desert. It was in the desert – barren, unpredictable, surprising – that the people of Israel learned the lesson of dependence on God in the simplicity of pure faith. Moreover the prophets saw the desert not only as the place of identity (as in Deut. 32.10) but also as the place of future renewal (Isa. 35.1-6). The desert testifies to the experience of God in terrible simplicity, it is the 'primal scriptural symbol of the absence of all human aid and comfort'.[5] Elijah in the desert, in Thomas Merton's words, 'becomes his own geography . . . his own wild bird, with God in the centre'.[6] For Jesus himself, the wilderness was the place of temptation and struggle (Mat. 4.1, Mark 1.12; Luke 4.1), and throughout his ministry he sought solitude in deserts and lonely places, instructing his disciples to follow his example (Mark 6.30). In the fourth century the deserts of Egypt and Syria provided the setting for that movement of purity and protest associated with the Desert Fathers who sought to maintain authentic Christian life in revolt against a compromised and worldly church. In the spirituality of the Desert Fathers, the concept of *hesychia*, inner silence, is without doubt the central theme. The cell was seen as a workshop or laboratory of unceasing prayer, of continual recollection of God. In effect, the desert itself was one great cell, and many testified to the healing power of its silence. However, the desert experience is filled with testimonies to the dangers of solitude for those who had not begun to penetrate the wasteland of their own hearts. For the desert is the place where idols are smashed, where illusions are unmasked, and where the human heart is exposed. It is therefore a place of great pain and upheaval, and some lose their bearings entirely, and become off-centre (the original, literal meaning of ec-centric). Yet only through such pain and upheaval can maturity come.

Secondly, the Dark Night. Silence is bound up with darkness. The Old Testament saw the vision of God, the God of Sinai, as an obscure vision, a knowledge of God in cloud and darkness, a knowledge of which one could speak only in metaphor and analogy. Here is the sharp contrast with the idols who can be seen and known directly, their forms discerned, their natures conceptualized, their names uttered, their territory and limits defined. The God of Israel, on the other hand, cannot be known in this way. So silence and darkness are central to the Judaeo–Christian understanding of divine revelation. The eastern fathers often speak of the 'divine darkness' and of knowing through 'unknowing', *agnōsia*. In Western Christianity it is expressed most memorably in the fourteenth-century work *The Cloud of Unknowing*.

> You will seem to know nothing and to feel nothing except a naked intent towards God in the depth of your being. Try as you might, this darkness and this cloud will remain between you and your God. You will feel frustrated for your mind will be unable to grasp him, and your heart will not relish the delight of his love. But learn to be at home in this darkness. Return to it as often as you can, letting your spirit cry out to him whom you love. For if in this life you hope to feel and see God as he is in himself, it must be within this darkness and this cloud.[7]

The author goes on to speak of the knowledge of God as a knowledge which comes through love, not through thought.

It is this interiorizing of loving knowledge, transcending the captivity of thought and of concept, with which St John of the Cross is concerned in his teaching about the dark night of the soul. Often mistakenly identified with depression and spiritual sickness, the dark night is in fact the way of illumination. In the journey of the spirit, St John teaches, the traveller moves fastest at night. The dark night is a process of dis-illusionment, of ridding oneself from illusions. The spiritual journey moves from the head to the deepest regions of the personality. Prayer becomes less our work, more God's work in us. We lose control, and at times seem to be on the verge of disintegration. Yet through this experience of darkness we come to see more clearly; we come to love more fiercely; we become more truly human. The path through darkness is in fact the way of integration.

It is in the framework shaped by Desert and Dark Night that the ministry known as spiritual direction took its historic shape. More will be said about direction in Part Two. Originating in the desert monasticism of Egypt and Syria of the fourth and fifth centuries, it was originally seen as a by-product of a life of intense prayer and silence, a gift of discernment which caused younger disciples to seek out a *pneumatikos pater* in the desert. It received its classic formulation in relation to contemplative prayer in St John of the Cross's writings where the primary role of direction is seen as discernment of the movements of the prayerful soul as it enters the dark night and makes progress towards union with God. Spiritual direction belongs then, historically and theologically, to the desert/darkness tradition. It is sought out particularly when people are moving from security to pilgrimage, from structured forms of prayer to more inward and receptive ways of praying.

In recent years there has been a revival of interest in spiritual direction. In the context of the consideration of silence, it is important to stress that one essential quality of the direction process is that of discernment. *Diakrisis* is the key word in the traditional literature. More than anything else, direction is about discerning movements, in soul and society; it is a ministry which is rooted in silence and attention, a ministry of vision and of clarification of vision. It is therefore a by-product of a life of contemplative listening.

I am sure that the great spiritual guides of the past would

have been horrified at the modern idea of training spiritual directors through courses, institutes of spiritual leadership, cassettes, and the like. They would have seen the spiritual director as one who emerges as an almost accidental side-effect of the life of prayer and recollection. However, Martin Thornton[8] has defended the notion of training and the professional approach to this ministry. The modern spiritual director, Thornton argues, must be competent in relating theology to the needs of individuals. Of course, head knowledge is no substitute for prayer and holiness of life, but it cannot be regarded as optional in the modern world. I believe Thornton is right, and he certainly speaks from the experience of having trained substantial numbers of spiritual directors in the Diocese of Truro over the past few years. He rightly emphasizes that 'spiritual direction was never a clerical preserve, neither was it traditionally reserved for the especially advanced or gifted'.[9] However, because the qualities and gifts of spiritual discernment are closely linked with a silent, reflective, and perhaps reticent personality, many actual and potential spiritual directors in parishes all over the world are not recognized or used. I believe that without recognizing and confirming such ministries of personal guidance, there will remain a disturbing and harmful gulf between the pulpit and the individual Christian. The spiritual director plays a crucial role in the unifying of solidarity and solitude, the connecting of the corporate fellowship with the individual needs of unique, but often perplexed and undernourished souls. It is, as Thornton wrote some twenty-one years ago, our greatest pastoral need today,[10] and I shall return to it later.

Finally let me suggest some practical ways in which silence and solitude can become part of our lives.

First, it seems to me very clear that, in an increasingly

25

fragmented and disoriented society, a society in which people and communities are being devastated and torn from their spiritual roots, we need to begin to shape new forms of community life which can survive the ever-encompassing barbarism, and nourish its victims. Alasdair MacIntyre ends his prophetic study *After Virtue*[11] with such a plea. The new dark ages are already upon us, MacIntyre says, the difference now being that the barbarians are in our midst and rule us. If we are able to survive these dark ages, we need a new St Benedict, someone who can help us to shape and foster communities of resistance and of vision.

In fact, there has been a remarkable revival of such communities of resistance and vision in recent years. More and more, the life of contemplation is linked with that of critical reflection upon the issues of the world, and resistance to its evil manifestations. What does seem urgent is that everyone who seeks to live a life of authentic Christian discipleship has a link with such a resourceful point. Each of us needs his or her own personal desert place. There must be a lived dialectic of contemplation and action, withdrawal and response, and this calls for actual physical places in which the contemplative dimensions of our lives can be nourished and strengthened.

No longer are such centres of solitude and critical reflection located only in the remote regions. The last decade has seen the growth of urban contemplatives, communities of Christian women and men who seek to live lives of prayer and silence within the urban scene. It was a movement predicted over twenty-five years ago by the Jesuit Jean Daniélou:[12]

> The Constantinian phase in Christian history is coming to an end ... The flight into the desert was a revolutionary innovation, lasting from the 4th century when St Antony inaugurated the age of monks; the withdrawal of the contemplatives from a world in which

Christianity was compromised into the solitudes where they might keep alive the faith of the martyrs. That age is passing – St Antony is coming back from his desert.

Today's quest is rather for the nourishment of the contemplative life in the midst of the modern urban deserts and wastes.

Secondly, we need to re-examine the priorities and facilities of each local church. A church should be a place of spiritual nourishment, a power house of spiritual growth, and this should involve the provision of space for silence and solitude. In every other area of life, there is attention (or at least lip-service) paid to ecology and the environment. In the area of spiritual formation, we need to take seriously the ecology of prayer. The conditions of the desert – a place of silence, of attention to God in simplicity and faith – should be made accessible in each parish community. How can we utilize our space so that it becomes a pressure and an impetus, rather than a hindrance, to the growth of prayerfulness? How can we help to create a healthy ecology of the spirit?

Thirdly, there needs to be a discipline of retreat. I do not mean the three-hour mixture of quiet and chat, but the deep silence of three to four days, undertaken at least once a year. A retreat needs to be accepted as a normal and necessary part of a maturing Christian life. Only through such occasional periods of concentrated and intense silence can that interior and continual sense of God's presence become a reality.

Fourthly, against the background of concentrated times of silence and solitude during the year, the pattern of daily times of silent prayer makes sense. Silence nourishes and feeds silence: the concentrated periods spill over into, and feed, the short times we manage to salvage from our day. But to create times of silent prayer and reflection each day calls for a sense of its importance and for a discipline. In

27

traditional Christian spirituality, the purpose of ascetical discipline was simply to create the external conditions in which prayer becomes more possible. It was part of what Monica Furlong calls 'pre-prayer'.

It is, I believe, a very serious error to oppose such spiritual discipline to spiritual freedom. On the contrary, the purpose of discipline is to create the conditions of freedom. Many years ago the Russian philosopher Nicholas Berdyaev made this clear. The only point of asceticism, he emphasized, is to restore us to reality, simplicity, wholeness; to bring freedom from disintegration; and to illuminate the world.[13]

Fifthly, we need to take seriously the provision of space for contemplative prayer and reflection within the public liturgy. There are at least two reasons why this is extremely important. It will contribute to increasing and intensifying the quality of public prayer as *true* prayer, not simply public affirmation or ritual gesture. But also is will help to overcome the unhealthy split between public liturgy and personal prayer, and restore to the liturgy its essentially contemplative character.

Sixthly, in theological training and in adult Christian education, we need to give high priority to cultivating the experience of silence and solitude. It is, on a purely practical level, in the interests of future generations of Christian disciples, to help to produce as pastors men and women of spiritual depth and insight. This means that we need to be exposing people at an early stage to the insecurity and wildness of the desert, to the journey beyond certainty which the dark night symbolizes. The pastoral task demands persons who have entered deeply into their own hearts, who have explored the wastes of their own inner desert, who have faced their own central darkness. No amount of charm, study or fluency in communication can be a substitute for this battle for the heart.

Finally, our aim should be the integration of silence and

speech, of solitude and social life, of prayer and action. It was this integration which was at the heart of all Thomas Merton's writing. It is what Brother Lawrence called 'the practice of the presence of God' and De Caussade 'the sacrament of the present moment'. The aim is to carry always within oneself a quality of inner prayerfulness and silence of spirit, *hesychia*. In the midst of daily work, play, love, or pain, we need to discover our desert, our fundamental and unique aloneness. In so doing we will begin to encounter the desert in others, for we will discover the truth in St Antony's words that our life and our death are with our neighbour. We will discover the essential interlocking of solitude and solidarity. We will recognize more and more the truth of T.S. Eliot's words of warning against those who 'neglect and belittle the desert'.

> The desert is not remote in southern tropics,
> The desert is not only around the corner,
> The desert is squeezed in the tube train next to you,
> The desert is in the heart of your brother.[14]

In an overactive world in which illusions are fostered and protected, rather than renounced, the resistance to solitude and silence is considerable. For in solitude there is both conflict and illusion, and encounter with the reality of God. In Nouwen's words:[15]

> Solitude is the place of the great struggle and the great encounter – the struggle against the compulsions of the false self, and the encounter with the loving God who offers himself as the substance of the new self.

But we prefer to avoid the conflict, and it is easy for our religion, our church life, to encourage this avoidance by giving us more to do. So, by piling one activity on another, we protect ourselves from any deep confrontation with self, and any deep encounter with God. Pastors and spiritual directors are not immune from this temptation to hyperactivism: they too run from the silence of their own selves, cultivating an illusory self-image of efficient pastorate and competent guidance. But their inner souls are dying through deprivation and undernourishment.

Without the dimensions of silence and solitude, the movement towards a unified society is doomed, for such a movement calls for a unifying of the personality also. The fate of the soul is intertwined with the fate of the social order. Thomas Merton often pointed to Gandhi as the great figure of the twentieth century who saw most clearly the interconnection between personal solitude and social health. He wrote of Gandhi:[16]

> This is his lesson and his legacy to the world. The evils we suffer cannot be eliminated by a violent attack in which one sector of humanity flies at another in destructive fury. Our evils are common, and the solution of them can only be common. But we are not ready to undertake this common task because we are not ourselves. Consequently the first duty of every man is to return to his own right mind in order that society itself may be sane.

3
Spirituality and Struggle

We have seen how spiritual maturity does not occur as a result of the accumulation of skills and techniques, but as a result of our being opened up to, and confronted by, realities which disturb and transform us: the reality of the Word of God, challenging, piercing, shaking us; the reality of the encounter with ourselves, with God, and with the depths in other people, through silence and darkness. Common to these encounters is the element of struggle, of conflict. We are formed through struggle.

The idea of struggle assumes a social dimension to the spiritual path. Everything that has been said so far takes for granted the fact that there can be no private spirituality. As Martin Thornton has written:[1]

> 'Private' piety, or even 'private' prayer, aimed at some sort of spiritual self culture, is unchristian, heretical, and a contradiction in terms: there is no such thing.

The word 'private' in fact is not a Christian word at all. The process of spiritual formation takes place within a world of wars and rebellions, of unemployment and strikes, of racism and oppression, of wealth and poverty. It is the relationship between private care and public struggle which is the theme of Peter Selby's important study *Liberating God*.[2] Selby rejects the false view of prayer as a form of self-cultivation.

> Prayer and meditation . . . are not some species of personal hygiene by which individuals isolate themselves

31

from anything that might ruffle the still waters of their inner tranquillity. It involves undertaking that inner struggle which is our personal share of the search for wholeness in its corporate living by the community at large.[3]

Selby goes on to point out that spiritual directors and members of the caring professions cannot escape the arena of public struggle, for they are as inevitably locked into the structures of society as trade unionists or boards of directors. However, they may seek to evade their responsibility for taking sides in public struggles by creating a peripheral religious zone for their activity. Thus

. . . the public arena is left to its own unchallenged devices while God is known at the edges by adherents who sustain themselves spiritually and offer to ameliorate pastorally the worst sufferings of the world's victims.[4]

So pastoral care is constantly in danger of deteriorating into ambulance work, or the dissemination of peace and inner satisfaction. But, Selby notes:[5]

The heightening of dissatisfaction, the arousing of a deep longing for the rectification of the social causes of distress – these do not appear very often, in print or in our heads, as goals of the pastoral enterprise.

Selby has, of course, correctly identified a phenomenon in spirituality which manifests itself in at least two ways: the identification of spirituality and prayer with the attainment of inner tranquillity and the cessation of conflict; and the identification of spiritual direction and pastoral care with the reduction of conflict and of dis-ease or maladjustment. Let me then enlarge briefly on these two aspects.

The spiritual life, and the experience of prayer which is its heart, is often assumed to be, at least ideally, a condition marked by peace and interior calm. There is a sense in which this is so. The Christian person, the person in whom Christ lives, should be characterized by a certain inner depth of peacefulness, and should radiate that peace to others. But there is a false peace which comes not from rootedness in God but from a kind of analgesic spirituality which seeks to remove the pains and conflicts both of the world and of the heart by dulling the consciousness. Marx correctly identified much religion as the opium of the people: today it would be more correct to see much spirituality as the religious equivalent of Librium and Valium. It was against such a false view of peace that the fourteenth-century Flemish mystic Ruysbroeck wrote scathingly when he spoke of 'the men who practise a false vacancy' and who are 'turned in upon the bareness of their own beings'.[6] Ruysbroeck describes the condition thus:[7]

> It is a sitting still, without either outward or inward acts, in vacancy, in order that rest may be found, and may remain untroubled. But a rest which is practised in this way is unlawful, for it brings with it in men a blindness and ignorance and a sinking down into themselves without activity. Such a rest is nought else than an idleness into which the man has fallen, and in which he forgets himself and God and all things in all that has to do with activity. This rest is wholly contrary to the supernatural rest which one possesses in God.

Ruysbroeck goes on to say that those who see the attainment of inner peace and tranquillity as the goal of the spiritual life, and who neglect the common life and the demands of charity and justice, are the most harmful and most evil men that live. For the life of prayer must never be separated from the struggles of humanity. The spiritual life is not a way of tranquillizing oneself against the anguish of the world.

As so often, it is Thomas Merton, steeped in silence, and nourished by the Word of God, who expressed so clearly for our day that Christian faith is 'a principle of questioning and struggle before it becomes a principle of certitude and of peace'.

> Christianity is not merely a set of foregone conclusions. The Christian mind is a mind that risks intolerable purifications, and sometimes, indeed very often, the risk turns out to be too great to be tolerated. Faith tends to be defeated by the burning presence of God in mystery, and seeks refuge from him, flying to comfortable social forms and safe conventions, in which purification is no longer an inner battle but a matter of outward gesture.[8]

There is, in fact, in prayer an essential element of struggle, of radical questioning, of discontent, of striving. In prayer we seek to see more clearly, and such clarified vision must bring with it a dimension of pain and anguish. In prayer we seek to understand more truly the workings of God's spirit, and such a quest must involve a dimension of questioning and of creative doubt. Prayer then is not quietism, but a yearning and a striving for the Kingdom in the freedom of the Spirit.

In his important book *The Night Sky of the Lord*, Alan Ecclestone speaks of disturbance and commotion as one of the characteristics of the Spirit.

> It is a function of the Spirit as Jews and Christians have known it to enter searchingly into man's house, and there to put questions; now like a breath, and now like a wind, to try all things that it finds there, to question their firmness to endure. The process in our own night sky is of near gale force winds.

> It is a delusion to suppose that the disturbing questions will, if ignored, go away, if suppressed, be forgotten, or that by hiding ourselves like naked Adam we can escape them. It is no less delusive to expect that we shall get comfortable answers to our questionings. To

live with our uncertainties is not simply a necessary facet of our education at all levels: it is the very truth of faith. To endure the sifting process of interrogation is the hallmark of discipleship.[9]

Only such a spirituality of questioning and of enhanced vision can survive the Marxist critique of religion as an opiate. Thus a test of our spirituality must be whether it makes us more aware of the realities of the world, and therefore more ready to respond to them, or not.

Linked with the view of prayer and the spiritual life as essentially analgesic and peace-inducing, is the assumption that in pastoral care and spiritual direction our primary concern is with the reduction of conflict and tension. This view is based on two false assumptions: that it is possible, and that it is desirable. In fact, the nature of the pastoral relationship is one which does not allow us to escape from inner struggle, but rather intensifies it. The pastor or spiritual guide will experience and absorb the conflicts in others; indeed, it is probably the fear of this experience which scares so many pastors away from too intimate relationships in caring. As Alastair Campbell has written:[10]

> Anyone who has entered into the darkness of another's pain, loss, or bewilderment, and who has done so without the defences of a detached professionalism, will know the feeling of wanting to escape, of wishing they had not become involved. Caring is costly, unsettling, even distasteful at times. The valley of deep shadows in another person's life frightens us too, and we lack the courage and constancy to enter it.

Yet pastoral ministry must include, and place a high priority upon, the intimate encounter with human beings in their inner striving for God. And if this encounter does take place, the result may not be tranquillity, but tumult, not the reduction of conflict but its intensification. This is

35

necessary if, as I suggested in the last chapter, maturity involves entering the desert and the dark night. The pilgrimage of faith will lead us through some ugly country. Spiritual direction which seeks only to alleviate distress and to comfort will be fatally inadequate for those who have progressed too far along the road to go back. They need solidarity and companionship, reassurance that they are still themselves, and, where possible, help in distinguishing the voice of God from the many conflicting voices within them. What they emphatically do not need is comfort, except in the literal, if now archaic, sense of that word as strengthening: strengthening for combat, strengthening for the movement of the Kingdom.

comfort that strengthens

The Kingdom of God is the key to the necessary new reformation in which prayer and politics, spirituality and social justice, mysticism and prophecy, will find their true harmony and interdependence. Christian prayer is Kingdom prayer: not the quest for inner peace of heart, but the stretching out of heart and mind towards the *shalom* which is inseparable from the justice and salvation of God. Over sixty years ago, Canon Percy Widdington predicted that the recovery of the centrality of the Kingdom of God as the 'regulative principle of theology' would bring about a new reformation compared with which the reformation of the sixteenth century would seem a very small thing.[11] The days of which Widdrington spoke are now upon us. Christians of many diverse traditions are recovering the wholeness of the Gospel concern both with personal *metanoia*, personal transformation, and with the struggle for a new world. They are seeing that the personal and the political are not opposites, and that both are embodied in the Kingdom symbol. The unity between the two has not been expressed better in recent writing than in Langdon Gilkey's chapter 'The political dimensions of theology' in his *Society and the Sacred*:[12]

The Kingdom does express to be sure the reign of God in the hearts of men and women; it does signal the stark opposition of God's love and justice to the historical world; and it does refer as well to the final culmination of history and of persons within history in God's eternal reality far beyond the bounds of space and time. Nevertheless, as its earthly analogue, a social kingdom, indicates, this symbol refers also to a redeemed social order, and ultimately to a redeemed history as well as to redeemed individuals.

The Kingdom of God is certainly more than a transformed social order: but it can hardly be less.

However, alongside this growing recognition of the unity of personal and socio-political transformation, there is also at the present time a reappearance of the old Christian heresy of otherworldliness. It is thirty years since Amos Wilder wrote that 'the characteristic heresy of modern Christianity, whether liberal or neo-orthodox, is the false spirituality of its message and life'.[13] The otherworldly spirituality of which Wilder wrote is once again a marked feature of much Christianity in the West, and is combined with an extreme individualism, the religious equivalent of free enterprise economics. In such versions of Christianity, the Kingdom of God is often reduced to a personal experience, a future hope, or a warm glow around the heart. Thus the American evangelical Jim Wallis comments:[14]

> Throughout evangelical training and experience there is no clear proclamation of the Kingdom of God. That is the single greatest weakness of evangelistic preaching today. By neglecting the Kingdom of God in our preaching, we have lost the integrating and central core of the Gospel. The disastrous result is 'saved' individuals who comfortably fit into the old order, while the new order goes unannounced. The social meaning of con-

version is lost and a privatised gospel supports the status quo.

However, if one major weakness of much modern Christianity is its neglect of the Kingdom of God, a second weakness lies in the area of Christology, the doctrine of the Incarnation. The truth of the Incarnation, of the taking of humanity into God, is the basis both of a materialistic, earthy and fleshy spirituality, and of a spiritually-based commitment to action in the world. The Incarnation emphasizes the 'carnality of grace',[15] the physical basis of spiritual reality, the presence of Christ in all flesh, the dignity and potential glory of being human. It is the Incarnation, the truth of the World made flesh, which drives us out to seek and serve Christ in the poor, the ragged, the despised and the broken. It is the Incarnation which makes it impossible for Christians to opt for a spirituality which despises the flesh, fears human passion, sexuality and warmth, and shuns the world of politics as squalid and contagious.

If many Christians still fear the political realm as a source of contamination, they do not thereby transcend political involvement. The 'non-political Christian' is invariably conservative, since to be 'non-political' is to uphold the status quo. Otherworldliness in theology tends, as a rule, to be allied with this-worldliness in politics since it deprives the believer of any theological or spiritual criteria by which to judge the structures of the world. Hence, from a doctrine of otherworldly faith, it is possible to move swiftly to an acquiescence in evil. The history of the Christian capitulation to Nazism still holds many lessons for our spirituality.

However, for other Christians, the last decade has seen a growing commitment to the causes of peace and justice. The growing opposition to the nuclear arms race and the corresponding search for a spirituality of peacemaking has sharpened an issue which was raised many years ago by Simone Weil. She wrote:[16]

> We should not think that because we are less brutal, less violent, less inhuman, than those we are confronting that we will prevail. Brutality, violence, and inhumanity have immense prestige . . . The contrary virtues, so as to have equivalent prestige, must be exercised in a constant and effective manner. Whoever is only incapable of being as brutal, violent and inhuman as the adversary, yet without exercising the opposite virtues, is inferior to this adversary in both inner strength and prestige; and they will not hold their own against them.

Weil was identifying the need to move beyond a simple rejection of violence to a disciplined strategy of organized love and peacemaking. Some years ago, one of the leaders of the National Front, a racist political party which had its main London base close to a church where I was parish priest, said, 'We have not invented racial hatred. We are organising it.' It is the sense that love, peace, justice, and the quest for a more human community need organization which has driven many young Christians from spirituality to politics; while the recognition of the depths of evil in individuals and structures has driven them back to renew their own inner resources and spiritual disciplines.

In every generation, there are certain vital issues which present the Christian community with a fundamental challenge to its spiritual integrity. If it fails to respond, many thousands of people may turn their backs upon it and seek God elsewhere. Such issues today include nuclear disarmament, the quest for racial justice, the response to the poor both nationally and internationally, the issues raised by feminism, and the challenge of Marxism. Within the Christian community, any one of these issues, perhaps all of them, will divide the church down the middle, perhaps in several directions. And so the tendency is to avoid such issues as divisive, preferring harmony to controversy; and, as we know, controversial matters are not conducive to church growth!

I believe this course to be profoundly mistaken. First, because it is untrue to the Scriptures and to the message of the Gospel. Nowhere in Scripture is harmony preferred to truth or to justice. The prophets attack those who cry 'Peace, peace' when there is no peace. Jesus promises not peace but a sword, not unity but division. Reconciliation is certainly the ultimate aim of the Gospel, but it is rarely the immediate result of its impact. The only people in the New Testament who are recorded as being reconciled as a result of the preaching of Jesus were Herod and Pilate.

Secondly, if we believe that the Holy Spirit is leading the church into all truth, then it should be possible and right for Christians of differing opinions to seek to grapple with those contentious issues lovingly, fearlessly, and prayerfully, and to seek a common mind. If the Christian community cannot do this, what hope is there for humanity? If we avoid these issues because they will divide our community, what kind of witness are we to the pursuit of truth?

It is neither possible nor desirable in our time that the way of sanctification should not pass through the way of politics. It is inevitable that it should, for pure ethereal spirituality is neither conceivable nor Christian. And clearly it is one aspect of the teaching and pastoral ministry of the church to support those who are struggling to relate the spiritual life to the demands of the political order. But is this task of guidance and support enough? If the church really is the 'pillar and ground of the truth' (1 Tim. 3.15), if it really is a provisional arm of the Kingdom, ought it not to be saying, in relation to divisive issues, 'It seemed good to the Holy Spirit and to us . . .' I do not believe that the church, internationally, nationally or locally, is preserved from all error, and it can make mistaken judgements. But it is surely better, after thought, debate and prayer, to speak on the basis of our present perception, than to remain silent in the face of great evil. For a silent church is not a neutral church, but one which takes the side of the power structure of the day. Martin Luther King, in his sermon 'A knock at midnight', stressed that the church is not called to be the servant of the state, still less its master, but rather its conscience.[17] That is a theological and spiritual task, one which calls for more and better theology. For if the church is to speak prophetically in and to the political order, it must do so on the basis of sound theology and profound prayer as well as accurate data and careful analysis.

Such a view of the church as playing a political role (rather than a 'politicized' role) is not new. Indeed it is the opposite view, that its role is only to do with individual salvation which is relatively new. As R.H. Tawney wrote some sixty years ago:[18]

> During the last two centuries, Europe, and particularly industrial Europe, has seen the development of a society in which what is called personal religion continues to be taught as the rule of individual conduct, but in which the very conception of religion as the inspiration and standard of social life and corporate effort has been forgotten. Possessing no standards of their own, the churches were at the mercy of those who did possess them. They relieved the wounded and comforted the dying, but they dared not enter the battle.

It was this personalised view of religion which was exported to, and intensified in, the United States, As the Constantinian era comes to its end, that view of religion too is ending. Churches are playing an increasing role in public affairs. The question now is: whose interests do they represent? Whose side are they on?

How is this connected with spiritual maturity? Many years

ago the Russian philosopher Nicholas Berdyaev predicted 'the appearance of a new type of saint who will take upon himself the burden of the complex world'.[19] Berdyaev sensed that holiness, perfection, maturity, could not flourish apart from the rough and tumble of the world with its constant threats to inner peace, and its constant presentation of the temptation to compromise. Holiness cannot be preserved in pseudo-innocence but only in struggle.

Christians who have become heavily involved in political struggles have become more powerfully aware of the dangers of innocence. In the New Testament, *nepios*, innocent, is sometimes used to mean under-aged. Thus Jesus thanks God that truth has been revealed not to the wise but to the *nepioi* (Mat. 11.25; Luke. 10.21). Paul uses it to mean immature babes in Christ (1 Cor. 3.1; Eph. 4.14). However, he distinguishes innocence in awareness from innocence in wrongdoing, urging his readers to be innocent in malice but to be adult in understanding (1 Cor. 14.20), a statement which recalls Jesus' words about serpents and doves (Mat. 10.16). Martin Luther King, reflecting on this text, urged Christians to combine 'toughmindedness and tender-heartedness', and so avoid the complacency of the do-nothings, and the bitterness of the hard-hearted.[20] This combination of clarity and vision and gentleness of heart is closely linked with the politics of non-violence and with the related issue of civil disobedience. But to practise the way of non-violence calls not simply for gentleness of heart, but for a degree of inner strength and maturity which is little short of heroic. That inner spiritual strength, once achieved and nourished, has tremendous power. In the words of the song used at Greenham Common, the Cruise missile base:

> You can't kill the spirit.
> She is like the mountains,

Strong and free,
She goes on and on and on.

The attempt to kill, crush or quench the spirit is, in biblical terms, associated with the collapse of prophecy.

In the 1960s we heard a great deal about the servant church. Today our urgent need is to recover the centrality of the prophetic church. Prophecy does not mean an easy mouthing of the latest fashionable slogan, an espousing, without pain or discomfort, of the latest safe cause. Prophecy means enriched vision. The prophets of the Old Testament are often called seers, rarely hearers. Their vision was a by-product of their contemplation. Prophetic witness must always begin with contemplation. Without that contemplative spirit, as Thomas Merton warned us, religion in the end always tends to become an opiate. However, a prophetic church, which sees visions and dreams dreams, which warns of judgement as well as celebrates life, will not simply emerge overnight. The prophetic ministry begins with isolated individuals and with small groups. Prophetic individuals plough a very lonely furrow. After their deaths, their churches – and governments sometimes – praise them, but during their lives they were an embarrassment and an irritant.

God has not ceased to raise up prophets in our day, and it is a function of a discerning church to identify them and to heed their words. But the church is also called, I believe, to nourish the small prophetic communities: communities committed to prayer and to politics, to contemplation and to struggle, to the vision of God and to the warfare with evil. In such communities, a real renewal of theology and spiritual discernment can take place, and is already occurring. In a broken world, in the new dark ages which are upon us, such communities can begin to play the role of the fourth-century desert movement in the beginnings of the Constantinian era. Today, as that era draws to its close, the church can begin to emerge from its Babylonian captivity into a new liberty to face new challenges. It will only be able to do this if it is spiritually mature, rooted in the Word, steeped in silence, and struggling in faith for the Kingdom of God and his justice.

In his *Letters and Papers from Prison*, Dietrich Bonhoeffer spoke to our condition:[21]

> Our being Christian today will be limited to two things: prayer and doing justice among men. All Christian thinking, speaking and organising must be born anew out of this prayer and action.

Part II
Spiritual Direction

4

Spiritual Direction and the Contemporary Climate

In Chapter 2 I suggested that the ministry of spiritual direction was being rediscovered by many people in our day. This rediscovery is taking place, for the most part, within a context which assumes the unity of spirituality and social action, of holiness and justice. I want, in this chapter, to consider spiritual direction as a deeply personal ministry within the body of Christ, and to begin by examining some widespread misconceptions.

It is not, as many suppose, authoritarian and despotic. Many Christians in the past, including some of the Tractarians, saw spiritual direction as a form of despotism, of spiritual slavery, and therefore rejected it as incompatible with Christian freedom. This seems to me to be a misreading of the tradition. The great teachers, from the Desert Fathers to Augustine Baker and St John of the Cross, stress the non-directive nature of direction. They emphasize the place of example. The director is to enable people to find the right way for them. The entire ministry of spiritual direction must take place within the framework of Christian freedom.

It is not a form of over-dependency. An excessive emphasis on 'spiritual fatherhood' is not in fact true to the mainstream tradition.[1] Indeed, there are frequent warnings throughout the tradition against excessive reliance. Spiritual direction is not a way of perpetuating immaturity. It is fundamentally an adult relationship.

It is not a form of ministry which is peculiar to the Catholic tradition. While the term has not until recently enjoyed widespread currency among Christians of other traditions, the reality of personal spiritual guidance was known to such writers as Bucer and Richard Baxter (who lays special emphasis on the pastoral care of the strong). However, spiritual direction was most strongly developed in the Catholic tradition where it was often linked with sacramental confession. Sometimes the two are confused. (See Chapter 7 on this.)

What then is spiritual direction? It is a relationship of friendship in Christ between two people by which one is enabled, through the personal encounter, to discern more clearly the will of God for one's life, and to grow in discipleship and in the life of grace. We can identify several characteristic features of such a relationship.

First, it is freely chosen. It is a charismatic, and not a sacramental or judicial, relationship. The concept of a spiritual director who is imposed upon one, whether by a seminary, bishop or other authority, is repugnant to Christian freedom. One seeks and freely chooses a 'soul friend'.

Secondly, one is free to abandon a director, and to end the relationship if and when it no longer fulfills its initial purpose. People outgrow one another, cease to serve and support one another, and there should be no sense of regret or embarrassment that this should be so. Spiritual direction involves a number of temporary, though important, relationships during the course of one life.

Thirdly, it is a relationship which is not authoritatian. Rather it is a mutual sharing in the Spirit, a mutual seeking after direction. It is therefore correct to see it as a special and intensified form of friendship.

Fourthly, it is concerned with the whole of life. It is wrong to see spiritual direction as only concerned with what is called the 'spiritual dimension' as if that could somehow be singled out and 'treated' in isolation from life as a whole. Such a view is not compatible with the orthodox Christian understanding of the human person. On the contrary, spiritual direction is concerned with the transfiguration of human personality in its wholeness.

Fifthly, it is a relationship involving help, support and teaching. Each of these elements is important. The director will often give direct help over issues or problems; he/she will endeavour to be a supportive presence and a source of strength and affirmation; and, from time to time, there will be the dimension of teaching and education. But the relationship cannot be seen as simply the sum total of these functions.

Finally, it is a relationship which calls for holiness and inner purification. It cannot be learned by the acquisition of techniques. Indeed technique without holiness can be harmful and destructive. This emphasis on the need for purification of heart and for personal sanctity is one which has implications far beyond the ministry of spiritual direction. It is part of a tradition, most fully developed in the East, which sees theology itself as a process of transformation. Theology is inseparable from the life of prayer and the quest for holiness.[2]

According to Christian tradition, the true and ultimate Guide of souls is the Holy Spirit. Scripture looks forward to a time when we shall not need to teach one another to know the Lord (Jer. 31.3). There is no warrant in Scripture for any approach which undermines the direct inner guidance of the Spirit, or which seeks to make the spiritual director into a guru. The guru in classical Hinduism certainly has similarities to the Christian spiritual director. But in the Christian way, Christ is the only Guru. However, spiritual progress takes place within the Body of Christ, and within this framework the human guide plays an important role. For within the Body of Christ there is a ministry of discernment of spirits. This ministry, recognized and affirmed by St Paul, assumed a special importance in the desert movement of the early centuries when the

49

Constantinian establishment threatened the purity and authenticity of Christian discipleship. It was out of this movement that spiritual direction emerged. From its beginnings it was linked with protest, with clarity of vision, and with purity of discipleship.

Ministry within the Christian community can never be seen in purely functional terms but must be seen in relation to sanctification. Sanctity is not a private possession, indeed it is not a possession at all. It is a work of grace in which we come to share the divine nature, and are nourished and built up by each other. So holiness and ministry are inseparable, just as holiness and justice are inseparable. Spiritual direction therefore has an importance at two levels: that of building up a sanctified ministry; and that of shaping a sanctified and consecrated people, a prophetic remnant.

There are at least three major reasons why the ministry of spiritual direction is of particular importance at the present time. It is important, first, because there is a lot of false spirituality about. Spiritual direction is very much concerned with *diakrisis*, discernment, and this involves the discrimination between true spirituality and false. There is therefore a critical and doctrinal dimension to direction which is particularly necessary today when we are in the midst of a revival of spiritualities of various kinds. The view that any spirituality is better than none is untrue to the Gospel and the Christian tradition. On the contrary, the biblical prophetic protest against idolatry and against false spirits is not matched by a similar protest against atheism. William Temple once observed that if people work with a wrong view of God, the more religious they become the worse it will get, and it would be better for them to be atheists. Indeed, from false spiritual paths atheism can be a real purification. Where the true God is not preached and worshipped, atheism may well be the last surviving fruit of the Gospel.

Today's spiritual explosion is confused and diverse. Much of it bears a close resemblance to early gnosticism. Many of the new spiritual movements are syncretistic, lacking roots in any authentic tradition, and they often rely on a view of humanity and of 'spirit' which is alien to biblical theology. Often the false polarizing of spirituality and social struggle which is common in many of the movements is mistaken for Christian orthodoxy. So the development of criteria of discrimination is an urgent task for 'where fertility is not matched by careful cultivation, it yields no livable human habitat, but instead the deadly luxuriance of swamp or jungle'.[3]

Among the trends in contemporary spirituality I would want to draw attention to the following aspects where careful discrimination and direction is needed:

(i)   *a resurgence of cults*, including occult groups, where religion is offered essentially as a private discipline, where salvation or enlightenment are seen in terms of the acquisition of techniques, and from which any sense of corporate social or political response is excluded.

(ii) *a revival of Christian fundamentalism*, a simplistic and unintelligent movement which combines intolerance and narrowness of vision.

(iii) *a revival of Christian anti-materialism* in which the incarnational and sacramental spirituality of the Christian tradition give way to the view that an emphasis on the transformation of this world robs people of their 'bridge to eternity'.[4]

(iv) *a revival of self-cultivation* where all the emphasis is on personal growth, a spirituality which is self-centred rather than God-centred.

The recovery of a ministry of spiritual discernment is

therefore of the greatest importance if false and dangerous paths are to be avoided.

The ministry of spiritual direction is of particular importance today. Secondly, because there is a spiritual renewal which needs, and is crying out for, direction. I cite as an example the charismatic movement. Here one has seen an upsurge of Christian experience which needs the guidance and direction of people who can help both to interpret the experience, and to integrate it into a wider understanding of the tradition. Without such guidance, the charismatic renewal could easily move, as in some places it has done, into a form of gnostic pietism, as well as keeping people stuck at a particular stage in development. The charismatic movement needs the breadth of vision of Thomas Merton, the experience of darkness of St John of the Cross and Simone Weil, the prophetic realism of Colin Winter and Alan Ecclestone, if it is not to become narrow and incestuous. At a conference in Chicago in 1976 there was a call for 'loving critics' of the charismatic movement who could offer 'a sobering influence and perhaps greater objectivity'.

> It is important that spiritual directors in the renewal have more than just the charismatic experience to recommend them. They best serve the renewal by being aware of the whole tradition of the church, and not just the slice of Christian history which began at the turn of the century in Kansas or in 1967 at Duquesne.[5]

They are many signs of renewal movements in the Christian world. But they will need careful guidance and direction so that they do not become isolated and cut off from the tradition. The quest for spiritual roots is a quest for corporate roots.

The ministry of direction is important today, thirdly, because there is a need to give spiritual depth to Christian social action. There has been a concern among Western

Christians for some years for what is termed the 'prophetic witness' of the church in response to trends in governments and in international affairs. Church and individual Christians have been led to speak out against structural evil in their nation, and this has provoked reaction from governments which feel threatened by such critiques. There are many signs of the growth of something resembling a new religious fascism in which the build-up of nuclear weapons, the growth of more represssive forms of legislation, the attacks on minority opinion, and the shift towards a more authoritarian and controlled society, are all seen as aspects of 'Christian civilization'.[6] In this climate, Christians who seek to follow the God of justice will find that they are increasingly marginalized.

Take, for example, the hardening of attitudes to the poor and the disadvantaged which has been so marked a feature of government ideology in both Britain and the United States in recent years. Many years ago the great Christian thinker R.H. Tawney observed that there was 'no touchstone except the treatment of childhood which reveals the true character of a social philosophy more clearly than the spirit in which it regards the misfortunes of those who fall by the way'.[7] A survey of opinion in the European Economic Community in 1977 showed that 42 per cent of people in Britain believed that the poor were poor through their own intrinsic defects (compared with some 24 per cent in the other member states).[8] There is no doubt that this contempt for the poor has been fostered by the philosophy of the British government since the late 1970s. Yet the truth that God is on the side of the poor is much clearer from the Bible than are most of the issues over which churches have divided.[9] Biblical Christians therefore can expect to be in serious conflict with the governments over this and other vital issues in the years to come. It is essential that this movement of Christian resistance is given adequate spiritual nourishment for the long hard battle ahead. Christian social and political action needs to be guided and nourished by the contemplative dimension, and by intense inner prayerfulness.

The ministry of the spiritual director is a daunting one. One is being called to share the deepest experiences of one's sisters and brothers in Christ, and while this is a great privilege, it calls for intensive spiritual preparation. For the spiritual director is called to be a person filled with, and yet giving way to, the Holy Spirit; a person of experience as well as of learning; a person of discernment and spiritual intelligence and sensitivity to the workings of God in the human person. These qualities are not acquired skills so much as parts of an outflow from a whole life of Christian discipleship and union with God. Indeed spiritual direction itself is a by-product of Christlike lives. Spiritual directors will often find themselves thrown into this ministry, feeling quite unprepared and ill-equipped for it. Yet in the very process of guiding others, we are guided, and may take comfort from the words of St John Climacus:[10]

> If some are still dominated by their former bad habits, and yet can teach by mere words, let them teach . . . For perhaps, being put to shame by their own words, they will eventually begin to practise what they teach.

5
Direction, Counselling and Psychotherapy

Great confusion has been caused by seeing spiritual direction in terms of a clinical model of sickness and distress. In recent years a number of writers have attacked what they variously describe as a 'hang up theology' or an 'ambulance syndrome', the understanding of spiritual life and growth in terms of problem-solving, crisis resolution, and so on.[1] Yet clearly the exploration of the frontiers of theology and the therapeutic disciplines has been of the greatest importance. Let me therefore begin this chapter by emphasizing the positive aspects of this exploration, and by pointing to three movements in particular.

First, the contribution of Jung and of the Jungian tradition of analytical psychology. In most of his writings, C.G. Jung was using categories of understanding and interpretation which seemed to overlap with those of theological discourse. He wrote of the loss of the spiritual life in the West, and of the need of powerful symbols through which one reached both the personal and the collective unconscious, and, perhaps, the divine. He wrote of the importance of myth at the very time when some theologians were trying to dispense with myths! If we lose touch with the world of myth, Jung argued, we cease to be fully human. With Freud, Jung saw the dangers of religion. But for Freud religion was itself an obsessional neurosis, intrinsically pathological. Jung turned the Freudian critique on its head, arguing that, while there undoubtedly is unbalanced, pathological religion, this recognition does not in itself deal with the question of whether all religion is essentially pathological. For spiritual directors, both Freud and Jung remain indispensable resources for the understanding of infantile, immature and damaging forms of religious life.

Secondly, the contribution of R.D. Laing.[2] Laing began to exercise considerable influence within British psychiatric circles through his work on schizophrenia and the family. From this work he moved on to explore the frontiers of madness and mysticism. Perhaps, he suggested, those whom we call mad are not ill but rather on a journey. Perhaps the 'mad' see more than we do, through having broken through to new dimensions of reality. Perhaps it is those whom we call 'sane' who are really deprived. True sanity involves breaking through the confines of the habitual ego, ordinary waking consciousness. It involves ego-transcendence, the recognition that the ego is only a small part of the total personality. Since Laing's work, there has been a movement within some schools of psychotherapy towards a stress on the 'trans-personal', a stress which has brought therapeutic work closer to the spiritual traditions.

Thirdly, the contribution of 'casework theology'. By this term, I refer to the pastoral counselling movement, in which the insights of casework and counselling are applied within a framework shaped by insights derived from Christian theology. In Britain this movement is associated with the work of the late Frank Lake and the Clinical Theology Association, Robert Lambourne, William Kyle and the Westminster Pastoral Foundation, and others. Before looking at the pastoral counselling movement more closely, let me draw attention to three points which are worthy of note. First, that the popularity of personal casework seemed to increase among Christians at the same time as professional social workers were questioning its value and moving towards a more political understanding of their work. Secondly, that what is often seen as a 'dialogue' between 'the church and psychiatry' is in fact very uneven. It does not take account of the vast majority of physicians, nurses and others working in the psychiatric field. Thirdly, some clergy have sought refuge from their own profound confusion about priesthood and theological activity by a retreat into the counselling field.

We are therefore concerned with a field in which there are important and valuable insights, but also certain dangers and confusions to be avoided, certain contrasts to be made. These can best be brought out by a consideration of the differences between pastoral counselling and spiritual direction.

It was in part the vacuum created by the collapse of any coherent school of spiritual direction which led many Anglicans in the 1950s and 1960s to jump uncritically on to the oncoming pastoral counselling bandwagon. In the 1920s and 1930s, there had been a school of directors and confessors, associated with such names as F.P. Harton, Somerset Ward, F.G. Belton and others. Writing of this school in 1963, Martin Thornton correctly observed that it represented a 'dying theological outlook'.[3] It was not surprising, therefore, that when the pastoral counselling movement developed, some people looked to it as a possible alternative model for spiritual direction. However, there are at least four areas in which pastoral counselling has differed from the tradition of direction as developed within the Christian church.

(i) Spiritual direction is essentially and centrally concerned with God, with the vision of God, with an understanding of the workings of God, and with helping human beings to attain union with God. Pastoral counselling, while it may take place within the framework of a Christian community, is not essentially concerned with theology or with belief. Nor can it become so without abandoning and betraying its function of counselling.

57

(ii) Spiritual direction is rooted in a Christian tradition which goes back to the monastic movement of the fourth century. While it must be flexible, and capable of adaptation to the needs of different ages, it can never abandon its rootedness in that historic faith tradition. Pastoral counselling is a relatively new discipline which draws from certain elements within Christian theology but which is less dependent on the Christian tradition as a whole.

(iii) Spiritual direction is not office-based but rooted in the life and practice of a sacramental community. Its locus is the church and sacraments. Pastoral counselling tends rather to be located in an office or clinic, and its links with the Christian community are less clear.

(iv) Spiritual direction is not primarily concerned with problem-solving or with life crises and states of emotional distress. It is not a ministry to the deeply troubled. Pastoral counselling tends to focus very much on problems rather than on long-term guidance within an ongoing and maturing spiritual life.

Of course, there are many similarities in approach between the two traditions. But those who see pastoral counselling as an alternative to spiritual direction would be wise to recall the words of the late Robert Lambourne, a priest and a physician, who in 1970 wrote of the limitations of a model of pastoral case which was based excessively on pastoral counselling and casework.

. . . the pastoral counselling called for in this country during the next twenty years cannot be built around a practice and conceptual framework derived from professional problem solving and prevention of breakdown. That practice and conceptual framework is based upon the clinical, medical and psychoanalytical models of the USA of twenty years ago, and it has proved inadequate . . . I believe that the pastoral counselling movement, most highly developed in the USA, must be seen as part of a too general assumption by society, epitomised by the medical profession, that we come to the good life by delineating problems, and then either avoiding them (prevention) or solving them. Pastoral theology has been over-influenced by the puzzle-solving view of human progress – a 'hang up' theology which fits only too closely with the medical clinical professional identity.[4]

Spiritual direction is about far more than the delineation, avoidance and solution of problems, and a casework or counselling model cannot do justice to it.

Ironically, about the same time that many clergy were adopting casework models for pastoral care, some therapists were looking afresh at the classical spiritual disciplines and traditions. Theodore Roszak has discussed the future of psychotherapy in relationship to the quest for spiritual identity and wholeness.

Our future image of human being, then, will be a strange, tense blending of the optimistic and the tragic: a study in paradox. We are optimistic in that we assume, not a radically 'fallen' human condition, but a whole and healthy nature at the core of us; not an original sin, but an original splendour which aspires to transcendence and succeeds often enough to sustain a godlike image of human being. We are tragic in that we see how easily, in our chameleonlike freedom, we misdirect that energy towards lesser goals, unworthy objects. The psychotherapy of the future will not find the secret of the Soul's distress in the futile and tormenting clash of instinctual drives, but in the *tension between potentiality and actuality*. It will see that, as evolution's unfinished animal, our task is *to become what we are*; but our neurotic burden is that we do not, except for a gifted few among us, know what we are. What is most significantly and pathologically unconscious in us is the knowledge of our potential godlikeness.[5]

59

Roszak goes on to argue that one of the most pressing needs of the present time is the rediscovery of the spiritual wisdom of the past, and he ends the passage cited above with these words:

> As all spiritual disciplines recognise, the will to transcendence may often concentrate itself in the 'dark night of the soul'. Disease means psychic tension, and psychic tension is the potential energy of the spirit.[6]

Roszak believes that psychotherapy is part of the process of 'unfinished animals seeking perfection', concerned not only with the excavation of neuroses, but also with the opening up of the personality. If this is the case, he argues, it is vital to promote psychotherapy for the essentially well person, and not simply for those whom we label as sick. Psychotherapy thus becomes a major conduit in our society for the transformation of human consciousness, and as such is itself undergoing a transformation into a spiritual and salvational discipline.

Many people will rightly say that they do not recognize psychotherapy from Roszak's descriptions, based largely on experience in California. Yet the central point which he has underlined is that the borderlines between spirituality and therapy are increasingly blurred – as they were in ancient times when, as Sir James Frazer observed, magicians and medicine men constituted the oldest professional classes. But the fact of blurred edges does not point to some kind of simplistic syncretism of disciplines. Religion and psychotherapy must ask critical questions of each other, and while the growing friendship between them has provided an atmosphere in which such questions can more easily be raised, the response to them calls for a higher degree of honesty than is often present in religious circles.

In a paper given in 1978 to a group of therapists and clergy, Irene Bloomfield identified three areas where, she suggested, religion and psychotherapy might be in conflict.[7]

(i)   Religion starts with an ideal towards which an individual must aim; therapy starts with the individual where he or she is.

(ii) Religion aims at holiness; therapy aims rather at wholeness, which involves confronting and coming to terms with the dark side or shadow. By its tendency to neglect the unconscious, focusing mainly on areas of consciousness and personal freedom, religious people may ignore the fact that, for example, many people simply cannot love.

(iii) Religion often does not encourage honesty by its stress on what 'ought' to be, rather than on what 'is'. Thus it may encourage repression of feelings, particularly in the areas of anger and sexuality.

I believe that Irene Bloomfield has correctly identified some areas of conflict, although they raise questions not only for the dialogue between religion and psychotherapy, but for a wider area of debate. For example, is religion idealist or realist? To what extent does religion involve belief in personal freedom, and to what extent does it stress human captivity, original sin, and so on? However, a brief response to the points raised by Bloomfield will bring out some of the key areas of importance for spiritual directors who seek to learn from the insights of psychotherapy.

(i) Undoubtedly much Christian spirituality has interpreted the way of holiness as a rejection of 'human nature'. So the more 'spiritual' one becomes, the less human one gets. But we must ask: does all spirituality do this? In a sense, the whole validity of spiritual direction as an enterprise rests on the assumption that it does not, and that an affirmative spirituality of human wholeness is possible. The association of holiness with wholeness and maturity has its roots in early Christian reflection on the consequences

61

of the incarnation. In the New Testament, the word *teleios*, perfect, is translated as 'mature' or 'adult' by several scholars. Of course, much spirituality or religiosity is a way of perpetuating immaturity. A central aim of spiritual direction is to lead people beyond the restrictions of such immature religion.

The therapeutic world is not free from similar kinds of dangers. It is all too easy to create an artificial world, a problem-oriented culture, a therapeutic ghetto, which protects its members from the wider culture in much the same way as does the ghetto life of the religious sect.

(ii) Again, undoubtedly much religion naïvely asserts a view of 'free will' which ignores the power both of the personal unconscious and of external forces. (At the present time, such a naïve doctrine seems to be more common among politicians than among theologians.) On the other hand, there is a long tradition within Christianity which lays stress on the 'demonic', on structural sin, and on the 'principalities and powers' of the fallen world. Indeed, some would accuse religion of being too determinist. If spiritual direction is to lead people to true liberation, true freedom, it must face the realities of oppression both within and outside the individual.

In reponding to such criticism, it is important to remember that much psychiatry and general medical practice is heavily influenced by a mechanistic and determinist view of the human person, with its excessive reliance on psychoactive drugs and external manipulation through chemicals. In opposing the misuse (though not all use) of mind-altering chemicals, psychotherapists and spiritual guides will find much common ground.

(iii) Again, much religion and much spirituality does not encourage people to be honest. Such a criticism should be received with gratitude, as should whatever help the therapist can give to the religious community in attaining a greater degree of honesty and truthfulness. It is one of the central purposes of spiritual direction to help the individual to attain to truth, to see more clearly, and to penetrate through illusion and falsehood. Without this fundamental concern for truth, however painful, the danger that religion becomes nothing more than an opiate remains very real.

The religious world may obscure the demands of truth and honesty in its own peculiar way, but the problems are not unique. The work of counselling, outside as well as inside the church, can become a way of escaping one's own needs and the truth about oneself, as David Brandon has written:[8]

> One neglected area . . . is the extent to which we hinder ourselves. Are there ways in which our practice of helping is used to stunt our growth as persons? Giving to clients can be a very effective way of concealing our deep-felt hollowness. I have frequently heard myself giving advice, guidance and love to people which I was completely unable to give myself. Helping and caring for others can be a very effective way of concealing desperate personal needs. It can conceal a need to control and even punish others. We may seek to be 'adequate in the face of the inadequacy of others'. Throughout most of my professional career I felt a continuing sense of fraud, of not being worth while, whilst trying to communicate the opposite to my clients.

It seems to me therefore that Irene Bloomfield has correctly recognized certain harmful and pathological manifestations of spirituality. The spiritual director can and must learn from the insights of depth psychology. On the other hand, it is necessary to avoid a 'sponge' understanding of religion in which the religious community merely absorbs the insights which come upon it from elsewhere. Let me therefore end this chapter with a

63

consideration of some of the ways in which the tradition of spiritual theology can contribute to the dialogue with therapy and the helping professions.

First, the tradition is rooted in materiality and in realism, in the earthiness and concern for the integrity of the human person which is basic to incarnational belief. At the same time, there is the ever-present danger that spirituality and spiritual direction veers off in the direction of some form of gnosticism, spiritual elitism, cut off from the common life of men and women. It is vital therefore that spiritual directors emphasize the material context of their ministry and the human character and quality of the workings of grace. Direction is an incarnational ministry, a social ministry, which occurs within the movement of the Kingdom of God. Like therapy and counselling, it must avoid that 'fear of flesh and politics'[9] which is the characteristic mark of the gnostic in all ages.

Secondly, the tradition holds together the knowledge of self and the knowledge of God. While these are not the same, they are inextricably bound up together. For the soul is fundamentally grounded in God who is closer to us than we are to ourselves.[10] This theological truth, stated so explicitly by Julian of Norwich, is at the heart of all spirituality. We begin not with a quest but with a fact: that men and women are deiform, created in God's image and likeness. The way to the knowledge of God must go through the way of self-knowledge. That is a central truth of spiritual theology as it is of many of the newer therapeutic approaches.

Thirdly, the tradition lays great emphasis on the place of conflict and crisis in the spiritual life. The 'dark night of the soul' and the warfare of the heart are necessary parts of the spiritual way, and no amount of study or ascetical techniques can replace them. In spiritual direction, what really matters is what happens to the soul when it becomes open to the workings of the Holy Spirit and abandons its need to preserve itself in peace and safety. Spiritual direction is not about the preservation of interior peace but about opening the doors of the soul to commotion and upheaval, and preparing people as far as is possible to respond to this necessary process by which alone true wholeness is attained.

6

The Prophetic Dimension in Spiritual Direction

It is still common for Christian writers to contrast prophetic ministries with ministries of pastoral care. Prophets and pastors, it is felt, do not mix well, still less does the fusion of prophetic zeal and pastoral sensitivity in one personal ministry. Prophets do not make good pastors, it is often claimed.[1] On a wider scale, there is a feeling that concern for social justice and concern for personal holiness and the inner life belongs to different religious traditions. Of course, it would be splendid if the two could be combined and held together, but, alas, it does not seem to be so. One either opts for prophetic rage or personal gentleness, justice or holiness. Undoubtedly, a good deal of personal observation would seem to support such a view.

Yet this kind of contrast does not seem to have very strong biblical foundations. The prophets confronted individuals, but can we say that they did not guide, that they were not pastors, that they exercised no ministry of spiritual direction? Certainly, if pastoral care excludes conflict, and is concerned only with sensitivity, gentleness, and non-directive counselling, perhaps the prophets do not come off too well. But the view that pastoral care excludes conflict is, as I suggested earlier, highly questionable. Indeed, pastoral care can be seen in terms of a series of conflicts and responses to conflicts. In the early Christian period, perhaps those individuals who stood closest to the tradition of the Old Testament prophets were the Desert Fathers, those wild and holy men of the deserts and mountains, who were in fact the first spiritual directors.

Moreover, there is no support in the Old Testament prophetic tradition for the separation between a religion of justice and a religion of holiness. The intimate connection between them is basic to the Mosaic Law and is reinforced in the prophetic writings. God shows himself holy in justice (Isa. 5.16). It is the contemplative vision of the holy and just God which leads these men to attack the oppression of the poor, the alien, the orphan and the widow. Their zeal for justice was rooted in their vision of, and struggle for, holiness.

The popular division between prophetic and pastoral ministry does not seem then to be biblically based, nor to have good historical support. Frequently movements of spiritual renewal combine the renewal of the inner life with a call to the pursuit of social justice. Nevertheless there remains an unease about prophecy within the framework of pastoral ministry. Richard Holloway, writing of what he calls the 'antithetic preacher', expresses something of this unease:[2]

He goes round like an enraged terrorist, throwing kerygmatic parcel bombs through the doors of the comfortable and efficient temples of Laodicea . . . He sets people's teeth on edge, and they often rise up and cast him out of the temple. Needless to say, the antithetic preacher rarely makes it in the suburbs, or only in those where there is a heavy concentration of masochists: then you get the contemporary equivalent of the medieval flagellant movement. But that's rare. Few people enjoy being whipped, even by a holy man, so the prophetic preacher tends to be an itinerant. He moves around a lot. He may not even hold down a permanent job, or he may be an associate professor in a seminary. He is more likely to be a curate than a rector, and if he is a bishop then he's almost certainly a bishop in exile. Angular and uneasy, he goes through the land, carrying on the Lord's controversy with his people, haunted by abandoned Eden . . . Harsh and often judgmental, he tends to make people feel guilty because he holds out to them, and often in himself exemplifies, an impossibly high standard. He is usually lonely, though he may have around him a small group of fanatical adherents. About him there is a whiff of the wilderness, an air from the desert, and a sense of disturbance that sends shivers through those who are at ease in Sion.

So the prophet appears in stark contrast to the sensitive, human pastor, treating people with patience, and treading carefully for fear of wounding the fragile soul. There is much truth in this unease, and yet the question cannot be left there. Spiritual direction must in some way reflect the prophetic witness and vision.

What then are the elements of prophecy? I suggest that six features are relevant to our present concern.

First, vision. The prophets of the Old Testament are often called seers, rarely hearers.[3] There was a visionary aspect to their apprehension of the Word. 'The word of Amos . . . which he *saw*' (Amos 1.1). The prophets are people of intense vision, clear perception and insight, and this vision is directly related to their proclamation. Clarity of perception precedes and shapes the prophetic utterance. However, there is the constant danger of trivialization and of visionary insight on the psychic or paranormal level which may lead either to a spirituality of sensational experiences, spiritual 'highs', or to a vicious kind of spiritual power lust and a need to control people. Roszak has warned of what he terms 'Flash Gordon religiosity'.[4] While vision and *gnosis* are essential elements in the prophetic tradition, the isolation of *gnosis* from love can be extremely harmful.

Secondly, and closely linked with vision, is contemplation. The prophets were people of profound prayer. The possession of psychic powers – which undoubtedly some of them did possess – is no substitute for waiting upon God. The God of the prophets was the God revealed in cloud and thick darkness, the God who had no truck with idols, the God known in the pursuit of holiness and justice. The contrast between the mystical life and the prophetic life is a contrast which is not known to the biblical writers, for whom the knowledge of, and union with, God was a unified whole.

A third characteristic of the prophets is accurate knowledge. The prophets kept their ears to the ground, knew what was going on. Thus Ezekiel is told to take a brick and portray upon it the city of Jerusalem before prophesying against the city (Ezek. 4.1,7). It is perhaps not stretching the image too far to see in this the injunction that we must know intimately the context before we enter upon a prophetic ministry.

Fourthly, prophetic ministry is a ministry of interpretation, involving discernment and discrimination. Thomas Merton summarized it thus:[5]

To prophesy is not to predict but to seize upon reality in its moment of highest expectation and tension towards the new. This tension is discovered not in hypnotic elation, but in the light of everyday experience.

The prophetic ministry takes place in the midst of common life, not apart from it.

Fifthly, a mark of the prophet which may seem incidental is eccentricity. Certainly the behaviour of the Old Testament figures was bizarre. Isaiah walked naked and barefoot for three years as a warning to Egypt and Cush (Isa. 20.2), while Ezekiel ate excrement as a sign of Israel's uncleanness (Ezek. 4.12ff). They were often written off as mad. This crazy wilderness eccentric element is more important than is sometimes realized. For these were people who were straining at the boundaries of consciousness where mysticism and madness meet, where sanctity can threaten sanity. The prophets often burn themselves out, often become unbalanced, and are usually disturbed as well as disturbing, While not all prophecy is ecstatic, undoubtedly the element of disturbance (*ek-stasis*) is a key element of the tradition. And clearly many of the great spiritual leaders of history showed similar signs of disturbance and loss of balance.

Finally, the prophets are intensely human people, and their appeal is to the humanness of their hearers, not simply to their religiousness. They appeal beyond the dictates of the religious law to the universal moral sense of humanity. They see the dangers of religion and of ritual, and oppose the obsession with liturgy at the expense of justice and mercy. Without justice and mercy, according to the prophetic understanding, worship is an abomination.

I want now to suggest that this prophetic dimension relates to, and is indeed central to, the full exercise of the ministry of spiritual direction in today's church.

First, the spiritual director is concerned with the attainment of spiritual discernment. Discernment of spirits is a vital element in the New Testament discussion of false spirituality, and it remains central to the understanding of direction from the Desert Fathers to St Ignatius Loyola. *Diakrisis* is in many ways the key word in the whole tradition, and it is a task which is closely akin to that of the prophet, for it is concerned with the attainment of a clear vision, of the insight which can discern between true spirituality and false, between reality and illusion, between paths which lead to maturity and wholeness, and those which lead only to destruction and death. We could say therefore that the central aim of spiritual direction is the achievement of such discernment. The enriching of consciousness, the enhancement of vision, the sharpening of awareness: these are of the essence of spirituality. If the eye is sound, the whole body is full of light. The spiritual director calls into question the concern of the religious mind with morality apart from vision, for, as Thomas Cullinan has put it, 'is it not far more important that we should see rightly than behave well?'[6]

Secondly, spiritual direction is inseparable from contemplative prayer. The bulk of the direction given by the Eastern Orthodox monks from the fourth century onwards was concerned with the attainment of *hesychia*, the condition of interior and perpetual prayerfulness, while in the West, St John of the Cross is largely concerned in his writing on direction with the movement of the soul towards deeper contemplation. Contemplation involves moving away from dependence on props and structures, being set free from idols and false images of God. And here too the work of spiritual direction is akin to that of the prophet, for the prophet sees idolatry as more threatening to true religion than atheism is. Indeed both the prophetic faith of the Jews, and the contemplative tradition of 'dark prayer', have at times been seen as atheistic by those for whom God is a super-object attainable by direct mental knowledge. The spiritual director, however, is concerned to help people grow away from such a limited view of God towards the deeper wrestling with the God of cloud and darkness, the hidden God of the prophets and the mystics. So in the work of contemplative prayer, the stress is on silence, on listening, on the 'way of ignorance' (*agnōsia*), and on the transcendence of thought and concept.

Thirdly, spiritual direction, like prophecy, seeks to perceive reality correctly and clearly. And this reality encompasses the structures of the world as well as of the soul. Thus Thomas Merton's insight into the forces shaping the United States in its social and political turmoil gave spiritual nourishment and direction to many of the activists of the 1960s. Merton saw that contemplation and the critique of social and political institutions were closely related, and that the ascetical disciplines of solitude and reflection should lead one to a deeper insight into and solidarity with the anguish of the world. Radical action begins with radical contemplation. So the spiritual director cannot ignore this essential task of helping people who are deeply involved with social and political action to see more clearly the realities behind the stereotypes with which their world is littered. Merton saw this task as an 'unmasking of illusion'. It is an aspect of spirituality which is never popular with the dominant power, for it speaks truth to power and uncovers the bogus and the sham.

Fourthly, spiritual direction is concerned to interpret, and to help others to interpret, the significance of events both within them and without. The director stands within the tradition of Christian insight and Christian critique within a changing world, entrusted with the theological task of seeing the events of the day *sub specie aeternitatis*, in the context of eternity. This task of interpretation involves drawing upon the personal history of the individual in his or her social context as well as upon the theological insights gained through brooding upon the Scriptures and the wisdom of the Christian tradition.

What, fifthly, of the crazy bizarre element? Spiritual directors do not, as a whole, seem to fit this description! Yet we should not be too quick to dismiss this dimension. John Saward's study *Perfect Fools*[7] has traced the concept of folly for Christ's sake from St Paul through to the present day. He shows how important was the figure of the 'holy fool' in both Eastern and Western monasticism, the very movements within which spiritual direction developed. Essentially the fool is a sign of contradiction, of refusal to conform to the dubious sanity of conventional society and its accompanying conventional religion. The fool symbolizes the dimension of scandal, of surprise, of unreasonableness, in the Gospel and the demands of discipleship. So in the work of spiritual direction there is an inescapable element of conflict, of spiritual warfare, of resistance. The director seeks to help nourish the inner resources needed in the struggle with principalities and powers, a struggle where often only the fool will enter the battleground.

Finally, the spiritual director, like the prophet, is concerned with humanity and with human progress. Spirituality which makes one less human, albeit more religious, is less than Christian, and is at odds with the incarnational basis of spiritual theology. Like the prophet, the spiritual director must look beyond the 'religious' world towards the fulfilment and transfiguring of human personality and of human society. As the prophet calls men and women back from the captivity of ritual and law to the human demands for justice and mercy, so the director must seek to guide people away from false spiritual paths which hinder maturity and inhibit progress. St John of the Cross is particularly hard in his attacks on those directors who actually encourage the prolongation of religious adolescence and immaturity. The purpose of the Dark Night is the attainment of a deeper integration of religion and life, of mind and heart. Its goal is the unified personality.

What may happen to spirituality from which the prophetic dimension has been lost? Such spirituality may well deteriorate into the quest for inner peace and comfort. Non-prophetic spirituality, spirituality without struggle, spirituality without justice, is notoriously popular in times of turmoil and upheaval. Ruysbroeck had much to say of it in the fourteenth century, and our own era is full of its manifestations. Spirituality can so quickly and so easily lose its contemplative, visionary dimension, and become a quest for salvation by technique, a matter of finding the right mantra or formula for instant enlightenment. Without the prophetic demand for sharpened perception,

73

the prophetic negative against all that would reduce the divine, spirituality can become a drug, a form of illusion, of clouding of consciousness, 'another resource of the culture instead of a resource against the culture'.[8] It is all too easy and too common for non-prophetic, privatized spirituality to become mere convention, as well as to lose its humanity and become nothing more than religiosity. True spiritual direction is concerned to discriminate and to avoid false paths, to create a healthy ecology of the spirit.

7
Spiritual Direction and the Practice of Ministry

Writing in 1963, Martin Thornton claimed that spiritual direction was the greatest pastoral need of the church, and he contrasted the growing manifestations of the need for such direction and the pastoral problem of how this need could be met, with the preoccupation of many pastors with how a demand for their services might be created![1] I believe that Thornton is correct, but there are some very major obstacles in the way of locating spiritual direction at the centre of our ministry.

In the first place, to do so runs counter to the prevailing models and emphases in ministry and in pastoral theology, and it can therefore be expected to meet with some resistance from those responsible for ministerial programmes, as well as by those at the receiving end of ministerial practice, those who, like the cannibal addressing a missionary conference, represent the point of view of the consumer. For much in our training and thought patterns is based on an organizational and managerial view of ministry. The pastor is a churchkeeper, a functionary who runs a show in competition with other shows. For this certain skills are required, but spiritual direction is certainly not one of them.

That this is so far as the United States is concerned is reinforced by examining the weighty study *Ministry in America* edited by Dr David Schuller and his colleagues.[2] For this study 5,000 members of 47 denominations were questioned about their understanding of ministry and its characteristics and qualities. Schuller noted the strong tendency in most churches to see the ministry in professional terms.

> Using the medical and legal professions as their models, this group desired both the technical specificity of content and the glowing status connoted by the word *professional*. A sense of inadequacy or inferiority was heightened as this group of ministers contrasted the more easily defined technical professions with the nebulous functions of 'ministry'.[3]

So we find that at the centre of the movement for professionalising of ministry is 'the concern to define as sharply as possible the competences demanded in contemporary ministry'.[4] This is not to say that many did not lay emphasis on the deepening of the spiritual life. But while most people regarded openness and the ability to relate to people as the most important qualities in the minister, with the ability to care for people under stress coming next, the specifically theological and spiritual dimensions did not come out very high in the responses of the laity.

> Laity generally consider it of less importance that a beginning minister seek to be a theologian in life and thought . . . For the most part . . . laity neither expect nor encourage clergy to probe deeply into theological issues. They assume that what needs to be known has been already learned at seminary.[5]

Again, in response to questions about the importance of seeking God's will through the guidance and ministry of others, the authors note 'the proneness of laity to view this stance as less necessary',[6] although pastoral counselling in states of emotional stress was seen as important.

In a report on one church, a study of 800 pastors revealed that the average pastor worked 66.7 hours each week, of which 5.5 hours were spent on church organization,

12.8 hours on hospital and parish visits, counselling and teaching, and 23.1 hours on less important areas. While clergy might have one view of the priorities in their ministry, they found that the expectations of them in the parish might be quite different.

> The message here seems to be that clergy feel called to ministry for one type of function, but are likely to spend their time and energy performing quite a different function. The care of souls is one thing. Making a parish a howling success is another.[7]

Now the professional model of ministry is very important in seeing how pastoral care has come to be seen in terms of the efficient use of resources. The classic study by James Glasse[8] drew attention to five characteristics of the professional: education, expertise, dedication, responsibility, and relationship to an institution. Others would add special knowledge and skills, and the existence of a clientele. But while such a model may well include spiritual direction among its list of 'skills' to be acquired, it is the skill, the technique, the ability to control a body of knowledge, which remains central to this approach.

It is worth drawing attention to a further aspect of this question. The concept of the church as a 'welfare church', an organization which cares for the underprivileged within a social structure which is not questioned, is almost certainly becoming popular again as economic and social policies in Britain and America create a climate of institutional deprivation. This model may also include 'spiritual welfare', but it is a model in which the church is seen as distributing services rather than enhancing vision.

There is a second major obstacle to locating spiritual direction at the centre of pastoral ministry. It will demand both resources and a reorientation which could throw established church structures into confusion. This is true in at least two areas.

(i) To place spiritual direction at the centre of ministry is to demand that ascetical and spiritual theology is placed at the centre of our life and activity. It is to call for a return to an older tradition of understanding of what theology is, a tradition which is sharply at variance with professional concern with precision and technical competence. In the words of the late Ian Ramsey, former Bishop of Durham:[9]

> Other disciplines will be judged primarily on the quality of their articulation; theology will be judged primarily on its ability to point to mystery. The only distinctive function theology can or need claim is that of being the guardian and spokesman of insight and mystery.

However, as we have seen, most of those who responded to Schuller's survey saw theology as unimportant and only related to ministry as preparation for it. The ministry of spiritual direction involves a view of theology as central, and as being of its essence rooted in prayer and contemplation.

(ii) To place spiritual direction at the centre of ministry involves reversing the sense of priorities in pastoral work. In a study in Britain in 1970, out of 33 clergy in a large industrial town, it was found that in an average working week of 62.5 hours, 27 per cent was spent on 'pastoral care'. But only an average of 2 hours 40 minutes each week consisted of 'personal consultations'. So unimportant has the care of individuals become. Evidence from elsewhere suggests that this is fairly typical. Yet if we are to take the demand for personal spiritual guidance seriously, we need to consider the effect of this on the present distribution of time and energy.

What then are the practical requirements of the kind of reversal of priorities that I have proposed? I would suggest that there are five which stand out in particular.

First, we need to shape the spiritual formation which

takes place in seminaries and in ministerial training programmes so that growth in the life of prayer and spiritual theology are placed at the centre. 'Prayer', Henry Nouwen has written, 'is not a preparation for work or an indispensable condition for effective ministry. Prayer is life; prayer and ministry are the same and can never be divorced.'[10] Yet my impression is that little attention is given to growth in prayer in many seminaries, particularly those which stand within the liberal Protestant tradition. If we are to provide the future church with pastors who are capable of guiding others, we need to place a very high priority indeed on training in prayer, on the practice of silence and reflection, on deepening the awareness of the presence of God, on helping people to understand the principles of spiritual growth, and on placing all theological work within a framework of worship and prayer. We need to be more concerned with sanctity than with the acquisition of pastoral skills and expertise. And this leads to my second requirement.

We need to recover a view of ministry which stresses the sacramental, charismatic, theological and prophetic roles more than the professional, managerial and organizational ones. The late Urban T. Holmes criticized the professional model of ministry on four main grounds:[11] (i) its acceptance of the modern concern with skills and functions as an adequate model of pastoral care; (ii) its neglect of certain key themes such as the sacramental, charismatic and liturgical dimensions of ministry; (iii) its assumption that the ministerial skills which it stresses are in fact wanted in our culture; and (iv) its tendency to exclude transcendence and mystery. Holmes pointed to priesthood as being essentially a ministry of illumination. We need to link this with our understanding of the vision of God as the central core of theological activity. The minister essentially points beyond the self to the glory of God. Like theology itself, the ministry is the guardian of mystery. Yet this idea is quickly lost in the obsession with technique. In the *Sayings of the Desert Fathers*, a monk asks Abba Joseph: What can I do beyond keeping a modest rule? The old man raised his hands to the sky and his fingers were like burning torches. 'If thou wilt,' he cried, 'thou canst be wholly flame.'[12]

Thirdly, we need to concentrate on building and nourishing a remnant, and to reject 'multitudinism' and statistical notions of church growth. A Gallup Poll of 1978 on the backgrounds, interests and values of the 'unchurched American' showed that churchgoers and non-churchgoers differed only very slightly in their beliefs. Growth in itself is not a value. In our concern with growth, we need to seek inner qualitative growth, the growth of the committed minority who can be salt to the world. If the salt loses its savour, how can its saltness be restored? The current concern in the church with growth seems mainly to be a concern with statistical growth. Yet David Wasdell has shown that such a concern, rooted in the concept of growth by addition, and in a 'radial model' of pastoral care, is a recipe for a self-limited church.[13] Once growth has reached a certain point it ceases. Moreover, on the radial model, pastoral care becomes increasingly difficult the further one gets from the centre, and beyond a certain point it becomes impossible. Wasdell suggests that we need instead to think in terms of growth by multiplication (that is, increasing numbers of small groups) and of a network model of pastoral care, by which we learn to minister to each other and nourish each other, thus releasing the pastor to be a resource and guide rather than a managing director. Writing out of his Latin American experience, J.L. Segundo stresses that the role of the church is to be a creative minority within the world.[14]

Fourthly, we need to build links between neighbourhood churches and places of spiritual leadership and nourishment. Parishes need to be linked with retreat centres and spiritual power houses, and these relationships need to be maintained and extended so that parishes can never become isolated units, cut off from the sources of renewal. A great deal of spiritual direction goes on in such centres, and for many people a relationship with a place is of as great importance and value as that with a person.

Fifthly, we need to establish a framework of ascetical discipline, an ecology of the spirit. An emphasis on space and on the physical environment is basic to good town planning, but in the life of prayer we just muddle along, as if the environment didn't matter. The context of prayer is even more important today when natural rhythms are dislocated and upset, and when many people find prayer unnatural. So there needs to be attention to personal rhythms of time, rest, sleep, discipline of the body, fasting (including 'mind-fasting', the rejection of mental over-crowding), and so on. Prayer is unlikely to survive at all except on the basis of concentrated daily times. For many people, it may not begin at all without the availability of spaces set apart for its nourishment.

If the ministry of spiritual direction is to assume a central place in the life of the church, the changes involved will be major ones. But unless such changes occur, 'church growth' may remain at the superficial external level.

Part III
Spirituality in Practice: A Study of Four Pastors

Personal Note on Part III

The section which follows differs markedly from the rest of the book in that it is much more personal. In 1983 I was asked to conduct the pre-ordination retreat for those being ordained in the Diocese of Birmingham. It coincided with the eighteenth anniversary of my own ordination, and with some inner wrestling with, and reflection on, the shape of my ministry. I felt that it would be useful to consider some of the priests who had been important influences on my own life, theology, and pastoral approach. I chose four priests, all dead, who, in very different ways, had made a major impression and impact on me. At least two of them were almost certainly never aware of how important they were to me.

It is my belief that, if we are to grow in understanding of the spirituality of pastoral care, and to make progress ourselves as pastors and people of spirit, we are likely to learn more from considering how it works out in practice in the lives of particular people, than from endless theoretical and generalized accounts of what should happen. I therefore make no apology for writing very personally of these four men and of what I hope I have learned from them. In reflecting on one's own priestly ministry and life, it is immensely valuable and deeply moving to identify those key influences on one's life which enabled some progress to occur; people who were put in one's path at the right time, and who enabled one to move a little nearer to holiness.

8

Brother Neville: Contemplative among the Poor

I first met Brother Neville, of the Society of St Francis, in 1958. I had arrived in London as a raw undergraduate, and made my way to the former brothel at 84 Cable Street where, since 1943, Neville and a small group of Franciscans had maintained a house of prayer and hospitality. The initial impact of the man was almost clinically disturbing. He was extremely thin, and wore an unbelievably patched and tattered habit which had clearly once been dark brown but was now showing signs of greening. Like Arthur Calder-Marshall, who interviewed Neville when writing the life of Admiral Woods of the Red Ensign Club in Dock Street, I was struck by his stubbly chin, and the fact that it was hard to tell whether he was growing a beard, hadn't shaved recently, or didn't know.[1] Neville Palmer, born in Prince Edward Island, was a very shy man. His normal greeting was 'How are you these days?', or sometimes just 'Good', followed by a nervous laugh. Neville did not waste time on much talk. Yet I sensed, at my first meeting with him, that this was a man who cared deeply about everyone he met, and who looked deeply into the human heart.

Neville had been a member of the Christa Seva Sangha in India, and, after returning to Britain had for a short time been a novice at the Community of the Resurrection at Mirfield. He was a contemporary there of Bishop Trevor Huddleston of whom he was always very fond and for whom he prayed daily throughout Huddleston's hard years in South Africa. But Neville found Mirfield much too bourgeois and affluent, later describing it as 'an old gentleman's club', and he left for the Society of St Francis. One got the strong impression that he found the poverty of the Franciscan houses a shade too genteel, and that he was much happier in the rat-infested house in Cable Street than at the more comfortable houses. The community sent him to begin their work in the Cable Street neighbourhood in 1943, and, with a few gaps, he remained in that neighbourhood until a few years before his death.

There is no doubt that Neville was the most awkward and most controversial of all the friars. He was a committed pacifist, a dedicated reader of *Peace News* (which he used to collect and pass around to unsuspecting guests during silent breakfasts), and one of the earliest supporters of the Committee Against the Hydrogen Bomb Tests and the Direct Action Committee against Nuclear War, out of which the Campaign for Nuclear Disarmament eventually arose. Neville belonged to the civil disobedience wing of CND, and was a strong supporter of the Committee of 100. He was particularly influenced by two members of the Committee, Michael Scott and the Quaker Will Warren.

In Cable Street, Neville was a legend. One could hardly imagine the street without him. At the time when I met Neville, Cable Street – or, more accurately, the western part of it – was the centre of London's juvenile prostitute world, as well as of the early drug traffic around the London Docks. It was the centre too of a criminal subculture which had formed around early stowaways from West Africa, and merchant seamen for whom the cafés and clubs with which the street was filled were an essential part of what made up 'Cablestrasse'.[2] Something of the life of the café society is reflected, in thinly disguised form, in the novels of Colin MacInnes who was often around the café next door to the Franciscan house, collecting material. Much of the property in the street had been condemned before the First World War. It was a violent street and a happy hunting ground for the Sunday papers. Ashley Smith, in a study of the East End, called it 'the filthiest, dirtiest, most repellently odoured street in Christendom'.[3]

But to Neville, Cable Street was home. He resented, and was hurt by, the hostile publicity. To him the western end of the street was a village, and its inhabitants – criminals, prostitutes, seamen, runaways, whoever – were God's children, and he loved them. Everyone knew 'Father Neville'. Many people who spoke little English did not know how to spell his name, and I recall letters arriving at the Franciscan house addressed to Father Nivel, Father Noble, Father Naval, Father Niggle, and, on one occasion 'Mister Fadernebble'.

What did I learn from Neville, and from the experience of living and working alongside him for three years? The first fact about him that was very striking was his simplicity of life. Neville's life was marked by an intense ascetic discipline. At times he seemed to take holy poverty to extreme and absurd lengths. For example, no food was ever wasted, and visiting students would be sternly rebuked for throwing pieces of burnt toast in the dustbin. (Neville would retrieve them and consume them on his day off!) There was an enormous tin of peanut butter which, according to legend, had been there since the end of the Second World War. Similarly, the sticky sweets, three of which were placed on one's pillow on Sundays and great feasts, seemed to have originated in years long past. Neville could often be seen storing bits of cold sausage and beetroot in a tin for days off. In the same way, every scrap of paper was used up. When I cleared the house before it was finally demolished, I found over 130 Lyons' Individual Fruit Pie packets on which he had written his sermons over the years.

Yet behind this eccentricity there was a profound sense of the goodness of the world and the sacredness of matter.

For Neville, simplicity meant living at the level of basic requirements, and finding there a joy, a freedom from possession, which was a true liberation of spirit. He was truly detached in the sense in which St John of the Cross used that much misunderstood term: a person of a non-possessive spirit, which enabled him to enjoy and experience the world freely. His was a spirit entirely opposed to the 'possessive individualism' which marks our culture and has defiled and corrupted the Christian community. Neville possessed nothing, and yet in his simplicity and detachment from things, he was at home in the world in a way which is only possible for the poor in spirit.

Secondly, there was an unshockability about Neville. He never really seemed surprised at anything. He was the kind of priest who, if someone confessed to having committed murder, would ask: how many times? His face rarely if ever expressed shock. In Cable Street, there was little he had not seen. But unlike so many Christians, including some who were working in that neighbourhood, he never dramatized or went in for histrionics. To him, it was all part of the way things were; and he smiled and plodded on. People felt they could tell him anything, however terrible – and they did. He had a tendency to understate everything and one of his favourite expressions was 'a little dispute'. The night-life of Cable Street was often marked by street violence involving large numbers of people with broken bottles and knives, and murders were not uncommon. Neville referred to most of these events as 'little disputes'.

Thirdly, I saw in Neville an utterly genuine identification with the neighbourhood and its people. For him, Cable Street was a piece of God's world in which he had been set, and he dedicated his life to the people of those streets. He was not in the slightest bit interested in concepts of 'promotion'. Even the word would have been meaningless to him. What could it mean, except being removed to another part of the vineyard, another place in which to exercise love and compassion? In a sense, Neville was always homeless. In the Letter to Diognetus, it is said of Christians that

> there is something extraordinary about their lives. They live in their own countries as though they were only passing through. They play their full role as citizens, but labour under all the disabilities of aliens. Any country can be their homeland, but for them their homeland, wherever it may be, is a foreign country . . . They pass their days upon earth, and they are citizens of heaven.[4]

Neville was like that: at home anywhere, and nowhere. After leaving Cable Street in 1963 he was sent to Sri Lanka to help guide an emerging Franciscan-style community in the Kurunagala district. Two years later he returned, telephoned me, and said 'I'd like a word about A – – – family in Half Moon Passage.' It was as if he had just been across the road, and was carrying on a conversation from a few minutes earlier.

A fourth feature of Neville was his care for the rejected. Above all else, he was a friend of the friendless, the helper of the afflicted. Two stories from my own parish experience illustrate the degree to which Neville had come close to people's hearts. In 1968, at about 3 a.m., I was outside a notorious all-night club in the Wardour Street area of Soho during a police drugs raid. A well-known dealer was arrested, and, as the police led him from the club, I recognized him as a former Cable Street figure from the late 1950s. His eyes met mine, and his only words were 'Hello, Father. How's Father Neville?' About ten years later, as a parish priest in the East End of London, I was helping to sort out some of the problems in a marriage which had broken up. The husband, a Muslim from Gambia, had told the local Citizen's Advice Bureau that 'Father Neville' was sorting out the problems. He had known Neville years earlier, but he had not been in touch for many years – and, to my recollection, Neville had recently died. I discovered that he was in fact referring to me whom he associated with Neville from the past in Cable Street. 'Father Neville' had become a generic term for all Christian ministers.

Neville cared for those whom respectable society shunned: winos, crude spirit drinkers, male prostitutes, many very tragic and broken people. He was their priest. I think he found respectable church circles quite difficult to cope with, and he felt very uncomfortable in them. Equally many conventional churchpeople saw Neville as a fool. He was in fact very much in the tradition of the 'holy fools':[5] unconcerned with his reputation or his image, prepared to befriend the disreputable and the depraved, irrespective of the consequences.

Finally, Neville was marked by an intense prayerfulness. He was a man of deep contemplative prayer. The tiny basement chapel was the heart of his entire priesthood, the source of his strength. I learnt more than I can say from Neville's example of prayer. Simply to be with him was a form of spiritual direction. In fact, Neville's 'method' of spiritual direction was simply to pray together. From him one learnt the value of long times of concentrated prayer in the very early hours. He was very much influenced by the French inner-city priests of the 1950s, such as the Abbé Michonneau, and by the Charles de Foucauld movement with its emphasis on the daily hour of adoration before the Sacrament. He was introducing people to the prayers and meditations of Michel Quoist some years before they were published in English. For Neville, inner prayerfulness and pastoral care were two sides of the same coin. Prayer flowed over into life, and life back into prayer, each nourishing and strengthening the other in a continuous dialectic.

*   *   *

These characteristics which I saw in Brother Neville are of continuing significance for all who seek to live the Christian life. We all need to learn simplicity. However, that is easier said than done. Not only are we ministering in a complex and fragmented society, but the complexity and the fragmentation go through the centre of us. Our lives are complex, and will almost certainly become more so. As pastors, we find ourselves torn apart not only by the conflicting demands of our ministry, but also by conflicts within ourselves. We need to develop a spirit of simplicity, a purity of heart, a singleness of purpose.

Simplicity is different from naïvety, immaturity and false innocence. It is a condition which comes from a refusal to be sidetracked by trivia; an avoidance of unnecessary clutter; an ability to see the wood through the trees; to discern the true amid the conflicting claims of illusion. Simplicity is therefore inextricably linked with discernment, the ability to maintain in the midst of turmoil and overcrowding of spirit a devotion to the inner light, the divine light.

The chief enemy of simplicity and of the simple light is distractedness and fragmentation of spirit. As pastors we are called to be light-bringers, little manifestations of the Christ light, and we can only do this if we are continually standing in the light, reflecting the light of the Lord. St Gregory Nazianzus sees this as the primary quality required of the theologian. The theologian, he says,

> ought to be, as far as may be, pure, in order that light may be apprehended by light; and . . . he ought to . . . have a calm from within from the wheel of outward things, so as not like madmen to lose our breath.[6]

Yet breathlessness seems to be one of the occupational diseases of pastors, and it is vital that God is allowed to shine in us and to preserve our breathing.

Like Neville, we need to learn not be be shocked. One of

91

the greatest hindrances to pastoral ministry is the image of the pastor as a fragile plant, needing only a harsh and boisterous wind to uproot and destroy it. The pastor is seen as a person who is easily shocked and scandalized, not fully human, one who needs to be protected from experiences and exposures which may disturb and upset a gentle personality: basically someone who is out of touch with the depths of human sin. It is important to break this down, not by a ridiculous exhibition of one's own fallenness, but by a warm, accepting, welcoming character. Whatever the rights and wrongs of the clerical collar, it is necessary to recognize that many priests use it to protect themselves against the world. As priests and pastors, we need to know that many people deliberately keep seven-eighths of their lives and experiences hidden from us. It is a sad commentary on pastoral history. Sometimes only some crisis in the pastor's own life can crack the remoteness from people which seems to be endemic in so many of us. Sometimes God seems to warm us by burning us.

Like Neville, we need to identify with the place in which we are set. One of the most wonderful things about Neville was the way in which he seemed to blend into Cable Street. Maybe his faded cassock was the same colour as much of the brickwork! So often clergy stick out in the most painfully anti-incarnational way. Everything about them cries out that they do not live there, they are just doing good to the natives. They are 'working among' people. (What a dreadful thing it is to be 'worked among'!) When I was a parish priest, I used to suggest to my curates that they spent the first month in the parish doing nothing except wandering around, familiarizing themselves with the map of the district, getting it into their system. Discovering the shops, the pubs, the street corners, the faces at the bus stops and park benches, absorbing the smells, listening to the neglected voices of the neighbourhood, feeling its pulse: these are vital prerequisites of good

92

pastoral care. You cannot effectively minister in unfamiliar
territory. Equally, you cannot minister to people whose
culture you ignore, even despise. It is a terrible truth that
some priests treat their parishioners with contempt.

Again, like Neville, we need to learn to care for the poor
and the wretched. 'This man drinks with publicans and
sinners.' 'If this man were a prophet, he would know what
kind of woman this is . . .' Jesus mixed in bad company,
made friends with disreputable characters, exposed himself
to every kind of criticism as a result. He seems not to have
been concerned with his reputation, unlike so many clergy
today who seem concerned with little else. If we are to
recover a genuinely Gospel ministry, we need to be less
bothered by our reputation and people's opinions of us,
and motivated more by the desire to seek out and serve
Christ in the broken, the lost, the damaged, the naked,
the sick, and the prisoner.

The truth that God is on the side of the poor is, as Jim
Wallis has pointed out, one of the first truths to be purged
from a church which has compromised with the world.[7]
Today, Christians who are concerned not only to care for
the poor, but to ensure that there should be no poor in the
land, find themselves swimming against the tide, faced
with governments which grind the faces of the poor, and
regard poverty as a character defect. Yet according to
Christian tradition, Christ is found among the poor and
lowly, while wealth and the accumulation of possessions
constitute a positive impediment to eternal salvation. This is
the clear teaching of the New Testament: God takes the
side of the poor, putting down the mighty, and exalting
the lowly. He is one-sidedly the God of the poor and the
lowly, and if we are to follow him and find him, we need to
be where he is, alongside the poor and lowly. Today we are
being called back to that New Testament truth by our
sisters and brothers in Latin America, that violent and
cruel subcontinent. Neville had grasped it in his violent

and cruel street. Amid the violence and cruelty, he found Christ, broken and oppressed, and he loved him there.

Finally, we need to learn the way of unceasing prayer. Prayer is being rediscovered today, but there is a danger that prayer and life may become separated, that prayer becomes a religious exercise. The world is seen merely as a neutral backcloth for the practice of private spirituality. The mediation of this false polarity of prayer and action remains a major pastoral work. The prayer life of the pastor is of fundamental importance if our ministry is to be an authentic reality, not just a job. For prayer and the life of the spirit is the one area where we can't go on faking it – as we can, to some extent, in parish administration, preaching and other areas. In prayer, we are stripped naked, reduced to confusion and bafflement. In prayer we enter the desert of the heart's pilgrimage, the dark night of the soul's journey. No authentic ministry can be built on prayerlessness. It is from our prayer that we discover the inner resources to be shepherds of the flock of God.

9

Stanley Evans: the Kingdom of God in the Back Streets

Stanley Evans was trained at the College of the Resurrection, Mirfield, in the 1930s, and it is typical of his ruthless attention to detail that in his archives in Hull University there is even the receipt – for three shillings – for his pre-ordination exams. His first curacy, like the rest of his ministry, was filled with controversy. Because of his involvement in the Aid to Spain movement at the time of the Civil War, his vicar did not recommend him for priesting. The Bishop went ahead against the vicar's advice, and so this extremely turbulent priest was released upon the Church of England. Though not quite released, for he did not hold a living for twenty years after his ordination. Though it was hotly denied, this was mainly because of his active involvement in the socialist movement. He was one of the leaders of the Russia Today group (which later became the British Soviet Friendship Society). He wrote one of the few histories of Bulgaria in English. He was leading visits of clergy and others to the USSR long before it was fashionable or respectable to do so. He was the *Daily Worker* correspondent at the trial of Cardinal Mindszenty, and followed the Communist Party line closely, preaching an eloquent sermon at the memorial service for Joseph Stalin. Throughout the 1940s and 1950s Evans edited a series of radical journals such as *Magnificat* and *Religion and the People*. Between 1946 and 1957 these contained detailed reports on the state of the Roman Catholic church in Yugoslavia, church-state relations in Poland, the church in Czechoslovakia, evangelicals in the

USSR, and translations of sermons by Russian bishops.

In 1955 he became Vicar of Holy Trinity, Dalston, where he edited *Junction* (named after Dalston Junction station), described as 'a journal of Anglican realism'. He was one of the early pioneers of the Parish Communion and Parish Meeting movement. In the 1950s at Dalston, the General Communion was followed by breakfast and discussion of the sermon, all features which were highly unusual at that period. With the attention to every detail, he faithfully sent copies of all his liturgical forms and even his parish magazines to the British Museum – possibly the only parish which took that obligation so seriously. In 1960 Evans became Chancellor of Southwark Cathedral where he set up the Southwark Ordination Course. He can rightly be seen as the pioneer of non-residential training for ministry in the Church of England. While he had moved away from the Communist Party after Hungary and the 20th Congress, he remained on the left and was Vice-Chairman of the Campaign for Nuclear Disarmament. He was one of the founders of the Christian Socialist Movement in 1960, and into this new body came the old Society of Socialist Clergy and Ministers of which Evans had been the leader and the principal intellectual force. He was killed in a car accident in 1965, but not before he had published several important books, including *The Church in the Back Streets* (1962) and *The Social Hope of the Christian Church* (1965).

I first met Evans in 1959 on a May Day march. My recollection was of an incredibly fierce man. He was thin with a long and wiry neck and a large Adam's apple which made him look rather like an enraged ostrich! In debate he was terrifying and merciless to his opponent. He ran Southwark Cathedral like a military academy. Once when worship was being broadcast from the Southwark Ordination Course, Paul Oestreicher (who had once been Stanley's curate and was then working with the BBC) emphasized to the students the importance of saying Amens gently and quietly and 'not like a machine gun'. Five seconds before they were due to go on the air, and when it was too late to stop him, Evans marched down the nave, and announced: 'Take no notice of what the man said. I want loud, crisp Amens, just like we always do them.' It was typical of him. One bishop was once heard to comment after Stanley's death that he used to fear death because he was afraid to meet his Maker: now he was more afraid of meeting Stanley Evans!

Although Evans was in the forefront of liturgical renewal, he was a ruthless critic of changes in the liturgy and in the canons and formularies of the church which involved, as he saw it, watering down fundamental Christian doctrines. Thus he wrote scathingly in 1961 of the new Revised Catechism which replaced the assertion that God the Father made 'me and all the world' by the assertion that he made 'me and all mankind'; which omitted the claim that God the Son had redeemed 'all mankind'; and which replaced the claim that the Holy Spirit sanctifies the elect people of God with the claim that he enabled 'me' to grow in likeness to Christ.

> So the process of eliminating the 'fellowship' of the Holy Spirit' in favour of a God-individual soul relationship, which began at the Reformation, now reaches its completion in the Church of England at a time when the whole world is being drawn to see that fellowship alone can save. How tragic and pathetic it is!

Evans ended his critique of the Revised Catechism by pointing to the main focus of attack in the church media, related to its omission of the Devil.

> The only public criticism of the revision so far has been in its elimination of the devil. Is it too much to say, that its compromise with 'the world', its failure to see all

mankind redeemed in Christ, its elimination of helping the poor from the work of a deacon, and the whole tendency manifested by these things, represents a retreat from fundamental Christian positions? And this is the very devil.[1]

Writing during the previous year, he made a similar attack on the revised rites of Baptism and Confirmation. Here he noted the removal from the revised liturgy of any renunciation of the world. Instead the candidate renounced 'the wickedness that is in the world'. Evans commented:[2]

The word 'world' has changed its meaning, and neither it nor its pomps are any more to be renounced by good Anglicans. At the Reformation the Church of England made enormous concessions to 'the world'. It has taken 400 years to have them finally enshrined in liturgical form.

Junction was full of this kind of polemic. In the final paper he wrote, an address to the Federation of Catholic Priests in Southwark which was never delivered personally because his death intervened, he spoke of the need for Catholic renewal. The paper is a brilliant exposition of the theology of the Second Vatican Council, a theology which he had held for the previous thirty years.[3]

What did I learn from Stanley Evans? The first and most powerful insight, which dominated his whole life and ministry, was his sense of the centrality of the Kingdom of God as the heart of Christian faith, hope and life. Writing in 1954, he stressed how basic Kingdom theology was to Christianity.

It is around this one basic concept that Christianity arose. 'The Kingdom of God' wrote Canon Widdrington, 'is the regulative principle of theology'. This teaching has been betrayed, side-tracked, forgotten, in one

Christian generation after another. But its roots are firmly planted in the official documents of the church, especially in its Holy Scriptures. Constantly it arises to trouble the waters, and to challenge the defeatism of those who in the name of Christianity refuse to confront reality.[4]

Three years later, during a lecture in his parish of Holy Trinity, Dalston, he referred to the divisions within the churches in terms of the interpretations of the Kingdom.

If we turn to the churches we find a two-dimensional split. On the one hand the historic split between east and west has been followed, particularly in the west by a denominational fragmentation which is today sustained by references to historical formulae the real meaning of which have been obscured by the passage of centuries. On the other hand, running right across these splits is the other one which, stated simply, divides Christians into those who believe in the coming of some kind of Kingdom of God upon earth and those who do not.[5]

Evans held the view that it was the latter split which was the most fundamental one. As one reads and reflects on his words in the 1980s, in the climate created by liberation theology, the theology of hope, and radicalizing movements among evangelical Christians, they have an extraordinarily prophetic ring. The division over the nature of the Kingdom and its relation to the structures of the world is indeed the crucial division among Christians in Britain and throughout the world. Evans saw this in the 1940s and 1950s, influenced as he was by the thought of Percy Widdrington and Conrad Noel.[6]

Secondly, I saw in Stanley Evans a remarkable combination of anger and gentleness. Undoubtedly Evans was a prophet, one who seized upon reality at its most intense point of potential change and orientation towards the new.

In many ways he was ahead of his time as prophets invariably are. But like all prophets, he could be quite unreasonable, difficult to live with, infuriating, impatient with stupidity, and at times extremely rude. And yet there was also a gentleness, an extreme sensitivity to people in need. I have rarely if ever seen anger and gentleness combined in one person in such a dramatic way. Part of the clue to this aspect of Evans's character was that he never seemed to bottle up rage, and therefore none of it was internalized. As a result, much of his fierceness was used up in debate and controversy, leaving behind a very tender and gentle pastor.

Thirdly, Evans was thoroughly opposed to churchiness and to the cultivation of the clerical caste and clerical culture. In his small but immensely valuable book *The Church in the Back Streets* he wrote of the effects of churchiness and clericalism on the individual pastor:[7]

> Only surrounded by clergymen can he be happy: the superficial *bonhomie* of the common room, or the gossip of the sacristy appears to be necessary to his salvation.

He was extremely critical of group ministries and of some of the recommendations of the Paul Report of 1963 on the grounds that they would encourage more and more clerical groupings, and by grouping clergy together would further cut off the clergy from the people. He feared and opposed any development which might make clergy and ordinands more churchy than they already were. He was similarly very critical of the seminary model of training and he encouraged and, through the Southwark Ordination Course, pioneered, alternative approaches to training for the ministry.

Fourthly, Evans had the 'common touch'. He seemed to know every pub in London, and wrote a history of the riverside pubs of which he was particularly fond. He was an intellectual and never pretended not be be. He strongly deplored what he called 'blokeage', a false and conde-scending attempt to identify, but he firmly believed that God sanctifies human pleasure and amusement, and that the pub was the natural place to meet one's parishioners. He often used to sing the words from G.K. Chesterton's *The Flying Inn*:

> God made the wicked grocer
> For a mystery and a sign
> That men might shun the awful shops
> And go to inns to dine.

For him, the pub was the place of relaxation and ordinary human comradeship. Yet it was all of a piece with his understanding of Christology. Shortly before his death he wrote about a visit to the Holy Land and of his reluctance to take part, and his words sum up his Christology and the incarnational basis of all his pastoral and priestly work.

> The fact that I have never had any deep desire to go to Palestine and kneel at the site of the manger at Bethlehem, or rejoice at the Cana where the water was turned into wine, or tread the bitter road to Calvary, is simply a reflection of the fact that I have been brought up to realise that Bethlehem could be the outhouse of any pub, that all water can be made wine, and that there are Calvaries enough to spare in London and New York. The essential theological point of the early Councils of the Church was their declaration of the universality of Christ, and for all that anybody can say to the contrary we have been brought up to accept this so that it never crosses our minds to doubt it.[8]

I think he overestimated the extent to which this understanding of the universality of Christ really had penetrated the Christianity of the West, but it certainly was at the heart of his own theology.

101

Finally, Evans's theology was rooted in his concept of the social nature of God. The central theological chapter of his major work on Christian thought is entitled 'The Social God'.[9] His zeal for social justice was rooted in Catholic orthodoxy. When a well-meaning young chairman of the Oxford University Humanist Group in 1962 thanked Evans for his unorthodox presentation of Christianity' (a phrase which he intended as a compliment), Evans interrupted his speech with a short lecture on the difference between orthodoxy and conventionality. In the peak period of what become known as 'South Bank theology', Evans asserted and reasserted his belief that any true and abiding Christian radicalism must be rooted in Trinitarian faith and in orthodox Christology. He held that the early Christological debates were of central importance in understanding the social and egalitarian nature of God, and of humanity made in his image. He was steeped in the early fathers, opposed Arianism in its ancient and modern forms, and saw the Blessed Trinity as the basis of a new world order.[10]

In our pastoral work today, the insights and character of Stanley Evans continue to speak to us. They speak first of the absolute centrality of the Kingdom of God as the heart of theology and of ministry. In Chapter 3 I wrote of the Kingdom as the key to the new reformation in the church. Evans held this view strongly, and would rejoice at the ways in which Kingdom theology has been rediscovered in our day. Pastoral care must be located within the framework of struggle for the Kingdom of God and his justice. Christians are called to be Kingdom people first, church people second.

Evans's insights and character speak to us also of the need in our lives and pastoral practice to integrate anger and gentleness. This task is one of the most important problems for contemporary spirituality. For undoubtedly Christians have real problems with anger and with the expression of conflict. Both our prayer and our relationships tend to be very genteel: they lack zeal, they fail to take heaven by storm. It is surely necessary to take the raw human emotion of rage, and to sanctify it. Only the person who has coped with rage can be truly gentle. Non-violence is only possible if one has faced the power of this rage. Yet many of us never cope with rage. It boils and festers inside us, while we present to the world a calm exterior, incapable of expressing the rage and violence within us. And so it comes out in twisted forms, or is turned inwards in depression and anxiety. At the social level, Christian gatherings are often depressingly polite, as if the expression of conflict were sinful or obscene. It is vital for our spiritual wholeness that we learn how to handle and use for God's glory the resources of rage and of tenderness.

We need too to learn the dangers of churchiness and of the kind of religiousness which cuts us off from the mass of the people. Evans saw the uselessness of the church's attempts to update its image without facing the deep issues of sincerity and commitment to humanity. As he wrote in 1959:[11]

> It is not just a question as all too many may think of the church 'modernising itself'. Young people may prefer snappier music, but they will not for long be fooled by it. Not snappier music, nor shorter psalms, nor basic Bibles; not cushioned pews, nor rocking parsons, nor jiving in the aisles; nothing but sincerity and truth will do.

True pastoral care must be based on a fundamental solidarity with and closeness to real people, a solidarity and closeness which the churchy culture may obstruct and prevent.

So we need to become more human pastors. Growth in ministry should involve a real humanization. Incalculable harm has been done by the image of the clergyman as cold, aloof, unbending, almost sub-human. Some clergy even seem to regard the cultivation of such an image as a necessary part of the sacerdotal insignia, and of their protective clothing from the world. Yet Christian priesthood is derived from the incarnate Christ who learned obedience through suffering (Heb. 5.8), and who raised humanity to share the divine life. Teilhard de Chardin, who was a significant influence on Stanley Evans, wrote of the need for more fully human priests:[12]

> To the full extent of my power, *because I am a priest*, I wish from now on to be the first to become conscious of all that the world loves, pursues and suffers: I want to be the first to seek, to sympathise, and to suffer; the first to open myself out and sacrifice myself – to become more widely human and more nobly of the earth than the world's servants.

True pastoral care is human care, rooted in the common life.

Most of all, pastoral care must be rooted in social theology. The whole concept of the pastor arose within the framework of a community – the flock. The pastor or shepherd is located within, and only makes any sense within, a community which is on its way to new pastures. So in the Old Testament there is a close link between the image of the shepherd and that of the Messiah who will initiate the *eschaton*, the new age. And all this activity and movement occurs within the world created by a God whose nature is social. Pastoral theology is therefore essentially social theology, 'for it is the will of the Triune God to inspire men to renew the world in such a way as to make it the perfect expression of his own being'.[13]

10

Hugh Maycock: Astonished at the Divine Beauty

Born in 1903, Hugh Maycock spent most of his working life in Oxford and Cambridge, apart from four years in Borneo just before and during the Second World War. He was a little man, who looked rather like a weeble. In his seventies, he still retained an amazingly childlike face, which symbolized his childlike delight in such things as sunrise. He was full of humour, and would burst into chuckles without warning, often in the midst of seminars or services. Hugh was one of the great clerical characters in both Cambridge, where he was Vicar of Little St Mary's from 1944 to 1952, and Oxford, where he was Principal of Pusey House from 1952 to 1970. His study in Pusey House had books everywhere, all round the walls, on every chair, and on the floor. Piled high among the books were many packets of Capstan Full Strength cigarettes which he smoked incessantly. All Anglican students in the university would be invited to lunch, followed by coffee in his room. At five minutes to two o'clock, Hugh would say 'Have another cigarette before *you* have to go.' What he meant was 'before *I* have to go', for at two every afternoon he retired to bed for two hours.

From Pusey House, Hugh retired to Canterbury, where he joined the staff of St Augustine's College, then the fourth-year college for ordinands of King's College, London, where all the emphasis was on pastoral and spiritual theology. Hugh became a sort of *staretz*, a wise old man, with no fixed role: a holy and entertaining presence which kept the place sane and laughing. We worked together on a school of prayer for three years. Hugh's opening words to the assembled students in 1971 were very memorable and quite typical of him 'Before I talk to you about prayer,' he said very seriously, 'there is something you ought to know about me. I think you ought to know that I am responsible for John Robinson's *Honest to God.*' The students looked baffled. Hugh went on, 'If you read that little book, you'll find that Robinson says that when he was at theological college – he doesn't say where it was, but it was Westcott House – he found the teaching on prayer, given by the chaplain, utterly useless and totally irrelevant. I was the chaplain. Anyway, having thought about it for some years, he wrote this book, which is really rather good. But I haven't changed!' Nothing could have been further from the truth, for Hugh was constantly changing, constantly learning, growing younger day by day. For, as he wrote in his notebook, 'in Christ we do not grow older but younger'.[1]

In Canterbury, Hugh managed to make his study a replica of the study at Pusey House, a room so packed with books, cigarettes and records that there was no room for a desk. The large window looked out onto the college quadrangle, and the sight of Hugh sitting in the window and always reading, was too much one day for the window cleaner who asked him about himself. After Hugh had described his life and how he spent his days, the window cleaner exclaimed, 'At your age, and you're still learning.' But Hugh was discriminating in what he read. Books seemed to fall into two categories, described by some of his favourite adjectives. On the one hand there were those books and writers whom he classified as marvellous, amazing, extraordinary; on the other, there were those which he dismissed as dreadful, absurd, ridiculous, out-rageous. Edwin Muir, Pascal, De Caussade, Julian of Norwich, and Harry Williams were all in the 'marvellous' category. From time to time he would discover some new author, and would immediately order all the published works over the phone, telling the bookseller how marvellous the author was. He became very enthused by a book by the American Anglican priest Robert Capon, and promptly ordered all Capon's works. 'Marvellous man, marvellous man', he used to say. On the other hand, Augustine, Thomas à Kempis, Francis Xavier, and a large number of modern writers, received scornful dismissal. He believed that *The Imitation of Christ*, with its encouragement of the view that one must withdraw from people in order to come close to God, had done great harm, and had distorted the whole understanding of spirituality. In a seminar on baptism, he suddenly launched into a devastating attack on St Francis Xavier, who he felt was largely to blame for the indiscriminate and semi-magical views of baptism with which the contemporary church was lumbered. 'That ridiculous man, charging round India with a hose pipe,' Hugh muttered. 'Ridiculous!' Sometimes he would change his views on people with amusing results. He was asked to speak at a centenary conference about Charles Williams of whom he was very fond. However, he got the year wrong, preparing the talk for 1974 instead of 1975. In the meantime he re-read all William's works, and, as he told the audience of Williams devotees, he discovered that he didn't really like him very much at all!

Hugh retired from Canterbury to be chaplain to the Sisters of the Love of God at their convent in Burwash, Sussex, where, after a few years, he died. The warden of the community, Donald Allchin, who had worked with Hugh at Pusey House and remained a very close friend, well summed up many people's feelings about Hugh when he said that they had found him 'one of the kindest, most humorous, most understanding, most loving and lovable human beings they ever met or are likely to meet in this world'.[2]

He seemed to exercise a ministry of pure being. He just

was. It was difficult to describe him in terms of what he *did*. A lot of the time he didn't *do* anything. 'I sort of potter about,' he said to someone who asked him about his role at Canterbury, 'and people come and talk to me.' 'What about?' asked the enquirer. 'God,' said Hugh, and then chuckled. He was a kind of resident guru at Canterbury, the wise old man, a cross between a Desert Father and a Zen Master – though if Hugh heard anyone saying any such thing, he would say it was 'ridiculous'. His priesthood was one of being around, being available. Students used to seek out Hugh for relief from the very cerebral and heavy approach of some of the other staff. Yet they found in him a profundity combined with humour and simplicity of manner. Hugh sat back and saw things whole, saw through the absurd and the silly. He moved slowly. (When the Sisters of the Love of God published their small devotional card which said 'Snails obey the holy will of God *slowly*' I wondered if they had Hugh in mind.) Often he would say nothing, but if he did speak, one knew that there would be no platitudes. Out of his 'pottering about' came a wisdom and a depth which was a source of great strength and encouragement to many. One of his favourite authors was Pere De Caussade who wrote *Self Abandonment to the Divine Providence* in which he used the expression 'the sacrament of the present moment'. Those two phrases were central to Hugh's spirituality: self abandonment to the will of God, and a sense of the sacramental character of every moment.

His ministry was marked throughout by a great sense of fun. He believed that heaven was a place of much laughter. After death, he once said, you go to sleep for a while, after which you are woken up by lots of laughing people who invite you to join them in their joy. Hugh's sermons were hilariously funny, and defied all the laws of sermon construction. They usually lasted twelve minutes and would often end abruptly with the words 'I think I'll stop there.' Once, a sermon on the 'dance of life', after entertaining his hearers with accounts of the development of the sacred dance, reached its climax with a reference to an Elizabethan poem, which, said Hugh, captured the theme of life as a dance better than anything else. The recitation of the poem was clearly the climax of the sermon. But Hugh then looked at his watch, saw that twelve minutes was up, and said, 'I was going to read it to you. There isn't time. You can look it up in *The Oxford Book of Sixteenth Century Verse.*' Sometimes his opening lines were as unexpected as his endings. 'Five years ago,' he began once, 'I was walking down the street in Cambridge . . .' Suddenly he stopped, blinked, looked at the congregation, and said, 'Did I say five years? It must be fifteen years now.' He then slowly took out his pen, altered the word, and, with no trace of self-consciousness, continued.

One of Hugh's most memorable sermons was on angels.[3] Angels, pure spiritual beings, were exactly the kind of creatures one would expect God to have created. Men and women, this curious mixture of psychophysical structure, were highly improbable. 'An angel would have much better reasons for doubting the existence of men than a man can have for doubting the existence of angels.'

Hugh's sense of the absurd and the ridiculous led him often to 'take the mickey' out of the pompous and the pretentious. He had a knack of bringing you down to earth. On one occasion, before a concelebrated Mass involving a bishop and many priests, as all the concelebrants gathered, vested and silent, in the sacristy, Hugh suddenly dug the bishop in the ribs, and, with a very serious expression but a twinkle in his eye, said loudly 'Do you think all this is a result of the Incarnation?'

Another central feature of Hugh was his sense of childlike amazement. In his diary which he kept during his time in Borneo (1939–40) he wrote of some of the early experiences of joy in his childhood: 'It seems to me now that those deep memories and ecstasies are by far the most genuine and unassailable possessions that I have and can never be lost or destroyed . . .'[4] In his later years Hugh still took a continuous delight in natural beauty. He would regularly get up early and drive to Herne Bay to see the sun rise. 'It's amazing,' he would say, 'amazing.' 'Amazement' and 'astonishment' were among his most frequently used words. In one of the few things he ever published, an article on conducting retreats for priests, he wrote that the job of a good cook is to astonish the stomach, and that the job of a good retreat conductor is to astonish the soul.[5] He saw astonishment as the basis of all religion: when men and women lost the capacity to be surprised and astonished, they could no longer be religious.

The psychiatrist Rollo May has defined authentic innocence as 'the preservation of childlike attitudes into maturity without sacrificing the realism of one's perception of evil'.[6] This process seemed to have occurred in Hugh. Undoubtedly he was under no illusions about the seriousness of human sinfulness and frailty, but, like the author of *The Cloud of Unknowing*, he held that there was always one part of the soul which never consented to sin. The divine likeness, shining within each person, was to him the most fundamental truth about human beings: sin was unnatural, an aberration.

Hugh was totally lacking in pretence. At times people found his honesty a bit unnerving, as when he used to forget the words of the liturgy. 'We are the Body of Christ,' he once said during the Eucharist. Then there followed a very long pause. 'In the Spirit we were baptised into the Body.' Again, a pause. 'Keep the unity of the Spirit in the, er, something of peace.' 'Bond', whispered the server. 'What?' replied Hugh. 'Bond, Father, Bond of Peace.' 'Oh yes, bond.' But 'the something of peace' was already part of Canterbury mythology.

At the centre of Hugh's day was sleep. 'When I wake up,'

he once said, 'if I'm in my pyjamas, I know it's time to say Mass. If I'm not, I know it's time for tea.' The period between two and four in the afternoon was always reserved for sleep. He had even been known, during day conferences at Pusey House, to introduce a distinguished speaker at 2 p.m., then leave and go to bed, returning at 4 p.m. to close the session. Hugh believed that human beings were created to enjoy sleep. If they didn't how could they ever cope with eternity, with that 'endless Sabbath'? Ceaseless activity with no place for rest was, in his view, a very bad preparation for death and for heaven.

A final feature of Hugh was that he was surrounded by novels. The theologians who influenced him were those with an imaginative approach, those with a sense of the poetic, and with a willingness to grapple with the realities of human experience. He had little interest in those systematic theologians who never read novels and never listened to Mozart. He suspected theology if it was not an integrated discipline, and had lost its unifying character as a reflection on human life and experience. His theological position was shaped by such figures as Dostoevsky, Hesse and Edwin Muir. Like Muir, on whom he wrote an essay in an Oxford symposium, he looked for beauty and creativity in the midst of 'the fields of charity and sin', for he believed that 'strange blessings, never in Paradise, fall from these beclouded skies'.[7]

Let me now consider these qualities and characteristics which I saw in Hugh, in the reverse order to that in which I described them, and draw out some general pastoral implications. First, the importance of reading novels, poetry, and literature which feeds and nourishes the imagination. Many clergy and pastors become extremely narrow in their experience, and deficient in their imaginative faculties. 'Keep up your reading', if it is followed at all, tends to be interpreted to mean the study of theology in a fairly narrow sense. But we need to read books which will nourish the human imagination, the total person, not just inform the ecclesiastical functionary. Through his novels and his music, Hugh became a very human kind of saint. (Can there be any other kind?) He would have identified very closely with some words of D.H. Lawrence:[8]

> It seems to me it was the greatest pity in the world when philosophy and fiction got split. They used to be one, right from the days of myth. Then they went and parted, like a nagging married couple, with Aristotle and Thomas Aquinas and that beastly Kant. So the novel went sloppy, and philosophy went abstract, dry. The two should come together again – in the novel.

In our concern that our theology should not become abstract and dry, a regular and rich diet of novels, poetry and music will be of the greatest help.

Secondly, the value of sleep. Sleep and prayer are closely related. Both call for a slowing down, a relaxed condition, an abandonment in trust. Yet many pastors seem to live their lives in a permanent state of semi-exhaustion. Not only is this a damaging state for the pastor's own ministry; it is also extremely cruel to the people who are affected by it. The well-known spiritual director Reginald Somerset Ward used to give his clients a threefold rule relating to prayer, sleep and work. As Hugh saw, the sleepless pastor can be spiritually harmful, and is ill-prepared for the sabbath rest of the people of God.

Thirdly, the spirituality of childlike amazement. If one of the main enemies of the Gospel is boredom, surely one of the authentic signs of the Spirit is the awakening and quickening of the imagination, of vision, of the ability to see. Hugh wrote, in his notebooks, of the contemplative spirit:[9]

Contemplation . . . is the common origin of all creative work – open to all, to every human being who wants to know, love, see and find out about God, the wild and lively God, creator of a wild and lively universe, with you and me and all the others in it – some of us not so wild and not so lively. By contemplation we renew contact with the ontological basis of our being.

Good pastoral care must be rooted in this experience of amazement before the wonder of the world and of its creator.

Fourthly, the importance of humour. Laughter is necessary to our sanity: a person with no humour is like an iron bridge with no 'give' in it. It is vital too that we learn to laugh at ourselves. Again, some jottings from Hugh's notebooks link laughter with the spirit of humility. He wrote:[10]

He laughed at himself because there was no trace of conceit or self-importance in him. He laughed at others because he retained throughout life a childlike unmalicious frolicsome quality. Here it seems is a humble man! Children are humble. How so? Children, I read the other day, have a hopefulness about their future and a disarming honesty. They look at nature with fascination, at their elders with bewilderment, at themselves with undisguised confidence. Humble. Yes, they are dependent, and know themselves to be that. They are not master of their fate or captain of their soul. They are trusting and capable of joyous responses, very vulnerable and very buoyant, spontaneous and gay. They play. They have not had enough experience to come, as adults do, to misleading conclusions and to lose their innocence.

It could well have been someone else describing Hugh himself, for all these characteristics were present in him to a remarkable degree. Sleep, amazement, and humour: all are qualities particularly associated with childhood, even with infancy. Adults so easily lose all of them, becoming restless, bored and serious. Yet the Kingdom of God belongs to the childlike, to those who do not take themselves too seriously, those who are not in control.

Finally, the ability just to *be*. It is often said that priesthood is being, yet our behaviour contradicts it. We become slaves of the work ethic, slaves of the tyranny of time. Yet if we are to redeem time, that is, not to become its slave, or to escape it, we need to develop an eternal perspective, a way of co-operating with God in trust and hopeful optimism. T.S. Eliot saw that

> to apprehend
> The point of intersection of the timeless
> With time, is an occupation for the saint –
> No occupation either, but something given
> And taken, in a lifetime's death in love,
> Ardour and selflessness and self-surrender.[11]

That, for Hugh Maycock, was the inner heart of priesthood: ardour and selflessness and self-surrender.

11
Colin Winter: The Breaking Process

Colin O'Brien Winter was born in Stoke-on-Trent of Irish ancestry. After ordination and a curacy in Eastbourne, he went to work in South Africa. In 1959 he was a parish priest in Simonstown where he brought about the racial integration of his congregation. In 1964 he was appointed Dean of St George's Cathedral, Windhoek, in Namibia, and, after the deportation of the bishop, Robert Mize, in 1968, Colin was elected the seventh Bishop of Namibia. He was one of the leading and most persistent critics of the apartheid policy of South Africa and of the illegal occupation of Namibia, and he spoke and wrote constantly on behalf of the oppressed people of Namibia. After his support of a strike of contract workers in 1972, he too was deported. But the diocese continued to regard him as their bishop, refusing to elect a successor, and for nine years he administered the diocese from Britain, first from a village in Oxfordshire, and later from a small house in the East End of London where he established the Namibia International Peace Centre.

During the years after 1972 Colin Winter made a tremendous impact on Christianity in Britain through his frequent meetings and talks all over the country. He preached and lectured in parishes and colleges, and met with individuals and groups in many towns and cities. He travelled throughout the world, speaking and appealing on behalf of the people of Namibia. He wrote poems and hymns too on behalf of the freedom struggle. One of the best known, sung to the tune 'Finlandia', is his hymn to freedom.

115

Namibia, enchained in tyrant's bondage,
Your people plead for freedom to be free
From rod and lash, from terror's sway a hostage,
To you, Lord God, they cry in misery.
How long, O Lord, how long shall evil triumph?
How long, O Lord, shall prisoners captive be?

Help of the helpless, comfort of the mourning,
Hope of the poor, the orphan's sanctuary,
They call for justice, shall that call be heeded?
They cry for mercy, shall they mercy see?
Arise, Lord God of Hosts, their one defender,
Smite tyrants' chains to set your people free.

Arise, Namibia, now your dawn is breaking,
United march to claim your destiny.
A people freed from racist domination,
Reborn in hope, destined for liberty.
Let freedom ring from every hill and valley;
Let justice stream for all the world to see.

To you, Lord God of Hosts, be glory given.
You gave us martyrs, give us victory,
The fire of freedom you alone implanted:
Children of freedom may we always be.
Namibia then one nation under heaven,
Upholding justice, truth and equity.

Colin died towards the end of 1981. His funeral, in a back-street church in Shepherd's Bush, and his memorial service, in a back-street church in the East End close to the Peace Centre, were joyful and inspiring occasions. During his last years, my parish was very close to Colin's home, and I had close contact with him. It was a great privilege to lay hands on him and pray with him shortly before his death.

People saw in Colin Winter a vigorous evangelical

radicalism. His zeal for social justice, for freedom for the people of Namibia, all his political concerns and struggles, were rooted in the Gospel. He never lost his evangelical passion, and he combined the best elements of a Catholic sacramental devotion and an evangelical witness and proclamation. I never heard a sermon from Colin in which he didn't involve the congregation in singing African choruses. The old ladies at Hackney Wick were initially taken aback when their vicar was away, and Colin turned up to celebrate a Thursday afternoon Mass, choruses and all! The children of St Clement's Notting Dale loved him, and, at his request, served and sang at his funeral.

Colin believed that the church in Britain had largely forsaken the demands and priorities of the Gospel. In his small but disturbing book *The Breaking Process*, published in the year of his death, he strongly attacked the church. All too often, he complained, it offered a Christ who was 'reduced to a figure of sentimentality, stripped of his passion, moral strength and outspokenness'. He continued:

> The fact is that the whole churches throughout the world have reduced the Gospel to the dimension of trivia. We allow people to substitute a few coins in a mission box instead of demanding the justice that the Bible requires for the oppressed. Instead of that involvement in the suffering of those injured by the injustices of society, as shown in the parable of the Good Samaritan, we allow the wishy-washiness of what passes for intercessory prayer which so often comes out like 'God bless everybody. Amen.'[1]

In Britain, he wrote, 'we have here a middle class church, served by middle class bishops and priests, most of whom are alienated by culture, lifestyle and background away from the poor. Certainly exceptions there are, but they are exceptions. The poor are not a priority for the church in England: the rich are!'[2]

117

Colin saw his vocation in Britain to help to 'free the church from the domination by the rich and to restore it (again) to the poor'. He urged the church to 'break with its long association with the rich'. This is what constitutes the 'breaking process' referred to in the title.

> There has to be a breaking process in which it is moved out of love and compassion to choose the side of the poor in our society. It must break with the rich, release itself from their control and their domination of its life and thinking. It is no good its pleading that it is neutral. In a class-divided society as unequal as ours is in Britain, such an argument is indefensible: neutrality in absolute terms is to opt for the powerful against the weak. But all this presupposes an understanding that we are a divided society in Britain and that poor and marginalised people exist here. But the church lumbers on as if this were not so, or, if it is, that it does not matter. It then chooses options which are irrelevancies as far as ordinary people are concerned. This inevitably leads to a church which is judged itself to be an irrelevance.[3]

For Colin, the Gospel made the most radical demands on individuals and on the Church, demands which would meet with resistance from those who were concerned primarily with security and safety. It called for a repentance, a renewal of heart and mind, which went right to the foundations of Western society.

Colin was a passionate man, a man of very powerful sexuality, a man who knew how to use his sexuality to draw out love in the frightened, the frozen and the friendless. He came out as a man from whom warmth and emotion came from every pore, he radiated passion, he was a fully incarnational person. I recall, with some amusement, a sermon preached in a theological college on the text 'If I tell you I love you, will you run away and hide?' As he turned and looked at the Principal, the man's eyes conveyed the horrified message, 'Yes, I will! don't you dare!' Colin came as a contrast to so many clergy who come over as repressed, carefully guarded, not to be shared, personalities. He simply poured out love.

Here too the personal and the political were united. In the midst of his international campaigns, Colin Winter never forgot the needs of individuals. At his memorial service at Stepney, alongside testimonies from exiles from Southern Africa, Palestine, Chile, and many parts of the world, was an old woman who had recently been rehoused from Whitechapel a mile or so down the road in Mile End. She had no idea who Colin was, except that he was the first person in her new street to invite her in for a cup of tea. Colin moved freely between speaking at the United Nations on behalf of Namibia, and visiting a sick child in the London Hospital. In 1975, after the collapse of the Salazar regime in Portugal, it occurred to him that perhaps the Portuguese authorities would no longer relate so closely to South Africa about people entering their territories. So he headed for Angola, which involved travelling through Namibia, his diocese from which he was banned. He was not allowed to leave the train and touch Namibian soil, but at numerous points he shouted to people from the train that he would be holding a confirmation along the Angola/Namibia border the following week. Crowds came out to greet and welcome him as he confirmed people through the wire-netting which formed the border, while he stood in Angola confirming people in Namibia!

Colin's last piece of sustained writing was *The Breaking Process*, a Lent book for SCM Press. It is a deeply moving and very honest book. He claims that all of us need to experience a breaking process. All of us need to be broken down before we can know the healing and transforming power of Christ. And we must not run away from this process, taking refuge in safe conventions and religiosity.

For Colin, towards the end, there was a real experience of both spiritual desolation and physical collapse. He felt very forsaken by the church, and his last few weeks were marked by a kind of loneliness which he used pastorally in a wonderful way.

In these last weeks, I think he learned more than ever before the need to lean on others. After his last heart attack, he went to convalesce with the Sisters of the Love of God at Fairacres, Oxford. They nursed him, loved him, and found him a very difficult patient. He learned, as a bishop, and a preacher and prophet of international repute, to be ministered to in his weakness by these enclosed sisters. In his last years too he was ministered to in a very impressive way by several people younger than himself: a young woman who gave him great support and care; a young layman who became a spiritual guide to him. He was humble enough to accept such deeply personal ministry from those who must have felt both very nervous and also deeply privileged to have been called to minister in this way.

Colin Winter's spirituality and discipleship are well summed up in some words he wrote in *The Breaking Process* about Jesus.[4]

The thing about Jesus was you either loved him or hated him; you followed him or plotted to kill him. Jesus really did tear apart his own society by his words, by his actions, by those with whom he associated, including harlots and some extremely unsavoury characters. Everything about him invited confrontation . . . There was nothing of the appeaser about Jesus. He did not practise the art of religious diplomacy. His language too showed no restraint; though it shone with gentleness and compassion for the sick, the broken, the rejected and unwanted, it carried all the sting of the viper when it was exposing the religious hypocrisy of the Pharisee . . .

Society's values were being exposed to the fierce gaze of the prophet, were broken in pieces to be replaced by the demands for total, self-giving love.

No one reading the gospel honestly could come away with a different conclusion: Jesus challenged the society of his day, exposed its meanness and sought to replace it. He was killed for so doing. Moreoever he never sought to apologise for this confrontation: he saw it as an inevitable consequence of faithfulness to the gospel.

These words about Jesus, read at the beginning of Colin's memorial service at St Peter's, Cephas Street, on 30 January 1982, could be applied to Colin himself who sought to follow in the steps of his Master. People either loves or hated him; he was a divisive figure; he associated with the broken and the outcast; he was undiplomatic and lacked restraint; and he saw it all as an inevitable consequence of the Gospel with which he was entrusted.

I have described some of the qualities which I saw in these four priests, and I want to conclude this section by trying to draw together some of these qualities and features and relate them to the requirements of a pastoral spirituality.

First, these four men were all Gospel radicals. Brother Neville combined a simple evangelical spirituality with a non-violent lifestyle, the best of St Francis and Gandhi. Stanley Evans based all his zeal for social justice on the central Gospel symbol of the Kingdom of God. Hugh Maycock, in a very different way, was able to pierce through conventional assumptions with a radical questioning, a prophetic insight and clarity of perception. Colin Winter too had a directness and a purity which was rooted in his love for Jesus and his vision of the Kingdom.

In our pastoral ministries, wherever they may be, we need constantly to be returning to our evangelical roots, constantly brooding on the Scriptures, constantly waiting on the Spirit. 'Radical action begins with radical contemplation.'[5] Without this dialectic of contemplation/action, prayer/struggle, our ministry may be a fine example of servanthood, but it will not be an authentic prophetic sign of the Kingdom of God and of the New Age. The servant church must never replace the prophetic church. Neville, by his insistence on the centrality of contemplative prayer; Evans, by his reiteration of the regulative principle of the Kingdom; Maycock by his life of amazement and astonishment: and Colin Winter by his direct Gospel-based preaching, were all able to hold together *diakonia* and *kerygma*, service and proclamation, the pastoral and prophetic dimensions of ministry.

Secondly, these four men were all people of tremendous passion, erotic power, and sexual energy. Neville and Hugh by their celibacy. Stanley and Colin in the expression of physical love in their families and flowing out to many people: they were all people of very powerful sexuality. They were not afraid of their sexuality, believing that it was the raw material of holiness, and that what Christ had not assumed he had not healed.

As pastors, we are entrusted with a Gospel of love, a Gospel of the Word made flesh. We are called to minister this incarnational faith as sexual beings. In no way can we pretend that our sexuality and our ministry can be disentangled, and the sooner we start to work through this the better it will be both for us and for our pastoral effectiveness. If we really believe in Incarnation, not simply as a once for all event, but as a process and a principle of life, then we must take seriously the 'carnality of grace', the truth that healing comes through the flesh.[6] It is through the human that we experience the divine, and as pastors we need to learn to offer our bodies as a living sacrifice to God so that they can truly radiate grace.

The solitary William MacNamara, in his two books

Mystical Passion and *Earthy Mysticism*,[7] points out that spiritual men and women need to become great lovers, and that this means seeing one's sexuality and one's sexual energy as the vehicle of the spirit. MacNamara describes the spiritual life as a life of being raised to white heat. Most of the time, however, we remain lukewarm.

> How distressing that the divine fury has not yet devoured me! Sacerdotal longevity worries me. It makes me suspect that I have not lived passionately enough, that I have merely warmed myself by the fire that Christ came into the world to ignite, but have not been consumed by it. It seems to me that the fierce and fiery men of God don't last long. They burn out quickly.[8]

That certainly happened to two of our four, but all were men who lived passionately and loved deeply.

Thirdly, they were all men who united the personal and the political in their life and ministry. The slogan 'the personal is political' became prominent in the 1970s through the women's movement. The critique of those who exalt political action above, and in conflict with, the demands of personal love and tenderness has also come from feminist writers.[9] What was impressive in these four men was that they seemed to hold together the immense issues of the world – the freedom of Namibia, nuclear disarmament, the struggle against fascism – with the small issues of small people.

Here is one of the most delicate and most difficult areas of pastoral ministry: how to confront evil in structures and in the prevailing values of society, and yet love and care for those who are promoting evil. It was a problem that faced me most acutely in my East End parish where we had the headquarters of a racist political party close to the church. How did one, at the same time, witness against racism, and show love and care for those actively involved in its organization? The danger is that we either become so person-centred that we become blind to the wider implications of our ministry, unable to see great issues because of our preoccupation with the specifics; or that we care so much about principle that we lose sight of persons.

As pastors, whether we like it or not, we are deeply involved in politics, both secular and ecclesiastical. The danger is that we become not simply political but also politicized. Politicization represents that captivity of the Gospel to the prevailing system and ideology which E.R. Norman sees as having occurred over the last two decades, but which has in fact been normal since the time of Constantine.[10] If we are to avoid being sapped into the machine of 'yes-people', we need to maintain this delicate balance of pastoral care and prophetic vision. Like Ezekiel we need both to sit astonished among the exiles, to sit where they sat, and also to prophesy, when necessary, against both the shepherds and the city.

Fourthly, these were all men in whom some kind of 'breaking process' had taken place. In Neville's case, it was a very literal break: he broke his leg in a fall in the snow, and never fully recovered. He became very frail, and spent much of his last few years in hospital. Evans was in a sense 'broken' by the church establishment, and for many years lived below the poverty line rather than compromise his principles. Out of this early experience of the wilderness and of isolation came a deepened sensitivity to the sufferings and isolation of others. Hugh, in 1974, experienced a very severe depression. It was painful and terrible to see this happy and cheerful man enter into a darkness of soul on which everything seemed to go, including God. For Colin, the final years in London were a 'breaking process', a time marked by physical illness and spiritual struggle.

St John of the Cross insists that it is only through some kind of spiritual crisis, in which we experience something of the desolation of Christ in Gethsemane and Calvary, that we can really grow in the Spirit. Through our wounds – or rather through Christ's wounds shared – others will be healed. Henri Nouwen has spoken of pastors as 'wounded healers'.[11] The best pastors are often people who have known great pain and inner wounding in their lives, and through these experiences have grown very quickly. Breakdown becomes breakthrough. And this is very much the heart of priesthood, for priesthood has to do with sacrifice, with inner offering, with sharing inwardly the dying and rising of Christ. The most important 'training' for priesthood takes place in the deepest recesses of the heart, in the spiritual turmoil, in the war with evil, in the struggle for inner integrity. No ministry which avoids that struggle can be other than superficial.

Finally, these were all men who knew the importance of friendship, and who were not afraid to lean on those close to them. One of the most desperate and tragic problems in parish ministry is that of the lonely priest. The situation described by Henri Nouwen is all too common.[12]

Being friendly to everybody, he very often has no friends for himself, Always consulting and giving advice, he often has nobody to go to with his own pains and problems. Not finding a real intimate home in his house or rectory, he often rambles through the parish to find people who give him some sense of belonging and some sense of a home. The priest who is pleading for friends needs his parishioners more than they need him. Looking for acceptance, he tends to cling to his counsellees, and depend on his faithful. If he has not found a personal form of intimacy where he can be happy, his parishioners become his needs. He spends long hours with them, more to fulfil his own desires than theirs . . . The paradox is that he who has been taught to love everyone in reality finds himself without any friends; that he who trained himself in mental prayer often is not able to be alone with himself. Having opened himself to every outsider, there is no room left for the insider. The walls of the intimate enclosure of his privacy crumble, and there is no place left to be with himself. The priest who has given away so much of himself creates an inexhaustible need to be constantly with others in order to feel that he is a whole person.

We can recognize ourselves so well in that description. It is so very important that we recognize our own need for love and for pastoral care. Who cares for the carers? Often very surprising people. If we are prepared to see Christ in the poor and the neglected, we need to be able to see Christ and receive his ministrations as delivered by others.

I have chosen four priests from among many who have ministered to me, and from whom I have received love, understanding and inspiration. To accept the grace of God through our fellow human beings is part of the incarnational and sacramental character of the Christian way. An adequate assessment of our own pastoral ministry needs to include the memory of grace received through the ministries of others.

12
Spirituality and the Renewal of the Priesthood

In the preceding chapters I have looked at the idea of spiritual formation through brooding on the Scriptures, through the practice of silence, and through struggle; at the ministry of spiritual direction as an important element within spiritual formation; and at the spirituality expressed in the lives of four priests. I want to conclude by some reflections on the implications of this for the renewal of the priesthood.

That there has been a crisis of confidence and confusion about roles among clergy in the Church of England has been commonly accepted for two decades or so.[1] Similar comments are made about the priesthood and pastoral ministry in other churches. The decline of the sacred, the rise of the social sciences, the growth of professionalism, are among the reasons listed for the loss of confidence about the clerical identity and role. However, it is important at the start to distinguish the role of clergyman/woman from the question of priesthood. My assumption is that the clerical role is concerned with a range of skills and functions which a person may assume for a time and may abandon. One becomes a cleric; one may cease to be one. Priesthood, on the other hand, is not a job but an identity, a condition, a sacramental state. One cannot shed it or be rid of it, though one may cease to practice certain functions associated with it. While it is possible to describe oneself, as an Anglican professor in Ireland once did, as 'a clergymen, but not to any great extent',[2] the priest is ordained for ever. The assimilation of all priesthood into the confines of the clerical caste is, in my view, at the heart of our problem.

The growth of the clerical profession has been closely associated with the rise of professionalism in general. The professional is marked by such characteristics as education, the possession of a body of expertise in a specified discipline or area, the acquisition of skills and functions which belong to this area, a relationship to an institution, a full-time salaried status, and so on.[3] More and more since the Second World War, and particularly in the United States, the clergy have come to be seen in professional, largely managerial terms. In a strong critique of the professionalization of the ministry, the late Urban Holmes pointed out that such a model led to the serious narrowing of ministry, and to the neglect of such areas as the sacraments, prayer, and the priestly role of pointing to the transcendent.[4] Recently other writers have stressed that 'pastoral care . . . is not correctly understood if it is viewed within the framework of professionalism'.[5] Priesthood is simply not understood, and in practice seriously distorted, when all the stress is on skill, function and the leadership role. The church is in grave danger when 'the symbol of the priesthood . . . is no longer the altar or even the pulpit but the desk',[6] and when the office becomes something you sit in rather than something you say.

But the professional model assumes that the skills and functions of the individual are in fact wanted and needed in a culture. What happens when the evidence suggests that they are neither wanted nor needed? Such has been the clerical dilemma in many places for years. So we have seen the retreat of many clergy into the 'caring professions' where they can at least feel needed and useful, earn their keep for a job well done, and retain something of the priestly role on Sundays and after office hours. We have seen too the growth of the ambulance, gap-filling view of ministry, a theology of pastoral care which is rooted in the notion of inability to cope. So the pastor becomes concerned primarily with the non-copers, with the broken and the casualty, with 'crisis intervention' and problem solving. And training for ministry comes to be increasingly taken up with the acquisition of skills in management or in counselling, in the expertise necessary for efficient control of the institution, and for efficient handling of personal problems.

Some clergy, perhaps the majority, seek to solve, or escape, the problem of identity by accumulating more and more jobs. Martin Thornton in the 1950s and 1960s spoke of 'multitudinism',[7] the pastoral disease by which the clergy rush about doing more and more, while the spiritual quality and intensity of the Christian community suffers neglect and ossifies. Thornton was particularly harsh in his criticism of concerns for numbers and for what has now come to be known as 'church growth'. He wrote in 1956:[8] 'The emphasis is numerical, membership is nominal; which inevitably means convention, respectability, Pelagianism, apathy and spiritual sterility.' Since then we have seen increasing concern with numerical growth, and clergy are judged (and in some places paid) according to their ability to 'build up the numbers'. The contention of this book has been that 'formation' and 'the building up of the Body of Christ' cannot be interpreted in terms of numerical increase but of inner spiritual maturity. And these two may well be in conflict: attention to one may actually impede the progress of the other. A church may grow numerically and decline spiritually.

But the effects of multitudinism on the pastor are disastrous. The incidence of clergy breakdowns, of stress diseases and exhaustion, of compulsive work leading to the resort to alcohol as a survival mechanism, present a worrying and growing problem. But what is perhaps more subtle and more dangerous is the undermining of those very qualities in priestly ministry which are vital for

129

spiritual growth. Monica Furlong, writing about the qualities she looked for in a priest, wrote:[9]

> I want them to be people who are secure enough in the value of what they are doing to have time to read, to sit and think, and who can face the emptiness and possible depression which often attack people when they do not keep the surface of their mind occupied.

The combination of overwork and the professional emphasis on skill and function undermines the inner reality of priesthood, and contributes to the process of spiritual decline. It leads to exhausted priests and starving communities.

There is no way out of this syndrome except through the rediscovery of the symbolic and sacramental character of priesthood. The priest is a God-symbol, in Austin Farrer's memorable phrase 'a walking sacrament'.[10] But our culture is one which does not see the world and reality in a sacramental way. The priest in such a culture therefore is bound to be a marginal figure, and no pastoral policy can be adequate which refuses to face the truth. The priest is a symbol of contradiction. 'A priest makes no sense at all in the world except to perpetuate in it the sacrifice of the Cross.'[11] To be a walking sacrament is to bear witness in one's body and life to the reality of God's grace mediated through matter. And sacraments, which are extended symbols, cannot be explained or translated into other terms.

The stress needs therefore to shift from that on skill and function to that on character and symbolic identity, to what R.C. Moberly called 'the inwardness . . . of priesthood'.[12] Thomas Merton wrote of his sense, when celebrating the Eucharist, of being taken out of his ordinary waking self into a different and more authentic level of consciousness and of personality.

Day after day I am more and more aware that I am anything but my everyday self at the altar: this consciousness of innocence is really a sense of replacement. I am superseded by one in whom I am fully real. Another has taken over my identity (or he has revealed it), and this other is of tremendous infancy. And I stand at the altar . . . with my eyes all washed in the light that is eternity and become one who is agelessly reborn.[13]

Merton is describing the sense of transcendence which is at the very heart of the meaning of priesthood, and the sense of daily dying and rising which is at the heart of Christian priesthood. Moberly saw the 'spirit of sacrifice' as the essential mark of the inwardness of priesthood. But this is only one aspect of the truth. In the Old Testament, the oldest part of the priestly work was to do with the oracles, the Urim and Thummim, and this was later extended to the Torah. A definition of priesthood purely in sacrificial terms is not true to the Old Testament perspective.[14] Priests were seen as guides (Jer. 18.18) and as sources of knowledge and instruction (Mal. 2.6-8). Only later did the sacrificial element come to dominate. It would be more correct to say that the earliest notions of priesthood were linked with the themes of spiritual guidance, illumination, and instruction in the divine law and path.

Of course, there is not a direct continuity from Old to New Testament. Nowhere in the New Testament is the Christian minister referred to as a priest. The Greek word *hiereus* is not used in the New Testament to describe the ministerial office, though priestly language is used both of Christ (Heb. 5.1-10; 8.1ff; John 17) and of the Christian community (1 Pet. 2.5-9; Rev. 5.10; 20.6). However, the word had entered the Christian vocabulary as a description of the ministry by the time of Polycrates of Ephesus in 190, and it is used widely by Christian writers from the Third Century, including Tertullian, Hippolytus, Origen,

Cyprian, Eusebius, Basil, Cyril of Jerusalem, Gregory of Nyssa, Gregory Nazianzen, and Macarius of Egypt. St John Chrysostom sees the priest as the *symbolon* of Christ.[15] But in asserting this, he is not introducing some new idea into Christianity, but rather reasserting the ancient understanding of priesthood within the Christian theological framework. For priesthood is human rather than specifically Christian, and it is rooted in the most ancient religious consciousness of humanity. Yet Christian priesthood represents a specific understanding of the priestly ministry which relates it to the Incarnation, death and resurrection of Christ. 'It is the office which ritually, inwardly and ascetically shares the dying and rising of Christ.'[16]

In the Anglican ordinal the priest is seen in a threefold way: as watchman, messenger and steward. First, as watchman, the priest is concerned with discernment, with clarity of vision. So contemplative prayer and social and political insight are equally necessary elements in the practice of the priestly life. Contemplative prayer because without this reflective, passive, receptive waiting on God in stillness and solitude, the 'inwardness' of priesthood will become dry and sterile. Ulrich Simon, in *A Theology of Auschwitz*, speaks movingly of the priest's role in the death camp, and relates it to his practice of silence.

> The priestly ideal uses and converts the nothingness which the world of Auschwitz offers. Here the priest's sacerdotal dedication encounters the vacuum with self-sacrifice . . . The priest at the camp counts because he has no desires of self-importance and gives life because he stands already beyond extermination. He is the exact opposite to the king-rat. The hour of darkness cannot take him by surprise since he has practised silence in darkness.[17]

The practice of silence in darkness is the essence of the

contemplative life. Yet social and political insight is also essential to priestly watchmanship: for to discern the signs of the times calls for a vision of the world which sees through its illusion and its falsehood. And such vision is the necessary preliminary to revolutionary change. The priest is concerned with revolution, in the literal sense *dunamis*, because priesthood is about dying and rising. Since the priest cannot exist in isolation from the community, that dying and rising must occur within the social and political context. Thus Herbert McCabe's image of the priest as revolutionary leader is not so absurd, and may help us to understand more of the nature of the priestly vocation of illuminating consciousness.

> The likeliest model for the Christian minister is the revolutionary leader: indeed the priest should be a revolutionary leader, but one who goes in and through what in today's terms is called a political revolution to a depth which today we call metaphysical or spiritual. This interpretation of the revolution in its ultimate depths *is* the proclamation of the Gospel.[18]

For revolution does not simply mean external rearrangements, but a total transformation, a *metanoia*, a new way of seeing and being.

The priest then is 'an agent for the illumination of the consciousness of the community he serves'.[19] The role of watchman involves the ascetical discipline of waiting upon God and learning to see the world clearly and freely. It involves a straining of the eyes towards the hills, stretching the confines of the mind beyond its normal conceptual limits. It involves the quest for transcendence. Holmes, in his valuable study *Ministry and Imagination*, deplored 'the loss of the central purpose of the Christian ministry: the mediation of transcendence'.[20] As the Latin word *pontifex* means a bridge-builder, so the Christian priest is to be a bridge-builder, one who, in Christ, mediates the divine realm, and points human beings towards glory.

The second element in priesthood according to the ordinal is that of messenger. The Greek word for messenger is *angelos*, angel.[21] That involves proclamation and instuction. So the priest is called to a theological task, to reflective study of the Word of God to wrestling with the Word, and to proclaiming the Gospel in the changing climate of our day. In Christian tradition the three principle angels, Gabriel, Raphael and Michael, are seen as ministers of proclamation, healing and warfare. Similarly, the priestly task involves these three spheres. The priest proclaims: hence the importance of preaching, teaching, clear writing, personal spiritual direction, and witness to the faith through a wide range of media and approaches. The priest heals: hence the importance of sacramental anointing, confession and absolution, intercessory prayer, and laying on of hands. Intercession was very specifically associated with priesthood in the Old Testament (Num. 16.43–8) and is central to priestly activity today. The healing power of intercession has been well expressed by Eric Hayman:[22]

> The intercessor spreads out over an ever-widening field the enfolding web of the love of God, and receives in his own person the anguish of the world's sorrow, its helplessness, its confusion, its sin. He meets the world's foulness with the purity of Jesus; he meets the world's rebellion with the obedience of Jesus; he meets the world's hatred with the love of the sacred heart of Jesus, and so takes his part in reversing the sin of the world.

Finally, the priest is involved in warfare: hence the importance of the daily struggle with personal sin, the ascetical disciplines of fasting and prayer, the confrontation with structural evil in the community. In all these ways, the priest is a messenger of God's love and justice. We can speak legitimately of the prophetic dimension of priesthood, for in the Christian dispensation, while prophecy is not in any sense restricted to priests, all priests are called to share in some sense in a prophetic ministry.

The third element is that of the steward of the mysteries of God. Here is the sacramental and sacrificial heart of priesthood. In the Roman ordinal the new priest is told:[23]

> The sacrifice of Christ will be offered sacramentally in an unbloody way through your hands. Understand the meaning of what you do; put into practice what you celebrate. When you recall the mystery of the death and resurrection of the Lord, strive to die to sin and to walk in the new life of Christ.

So the priest who celebrates the Eucharist is to become a eucharistic person, a walking sacrament of Christ's sacrificial presence. As in the Eucharist there is both awe and intimacy, so in the priestly life there is both an exalted dignity and a common humanity. We can say, with the twelfth-century writer: 'O revered dignity of priests, in whose hands the Son of God is incarnated as in the Virgin's womb!'[24] Yet that priest is also a broken, vulnerable, human being, and this vulnerability 'lies at the heart of effective priesthood'.[25]

The renewal of the priesthood is thus not primarily a matter of better organization, rationalizing of resources, improved techniques, or higher standards of training, but a matter of recovering the sacramental and symbolic character of priesthood. And here clericalism stands in the way of renewal. For clericalism has narrowed the understanding of priesthood to an educated professional cadre, which, in Britain, is also white, male and middle class. In addition, clericalism has distorted the essential humanity of the priesthood by setting apart the clergy in a uniformed caste. Martin Thornton has spoken of 'clerical monophysitism'.[26] The monophysites were those who claimed that there was only one nature in Christ, the divine, and that the humanity was swallowed up in it. Clericalism has helped to undermine that human solidarity with the common people which is of the essence of priesthood and of incarnational religion. Moreover, clericalism has located the clergy firmly within the institutional church framework so that they are seen as servants and officials of the institution. But priesthood is to do not only with the church but with humanity, and with the Kingdom of God as a vision for the human race. The church is 'a mobile and temporary phenomenon in history',[27] not the end of existence. Yet clergy are seen, and trained, to be church-keepers, parish functionaries, officials of the establishment and of the status quo. Not only is this a narrow and inadequate view of priesthood: it is difficult to see how the central task of the priest as one who illumines and who symbolizes the divine can be pursued within this essentially managerial model.

Spirituality is not simply a preparation for good pastoral care and good priesthood, a technique for doing some job better. It is the inner reality of priesthood and pastorate, it is the integrated and lived theology of holiness and liberation, the heart of sacramental action, the flesh and blood of the pastoral life. All pastoral work and action must be rooted in, and take its meaning and life from, the inner life of the spirit. All priesthood must find its identity, its central meaning, in that inner solidarity with Christ which is the core of the contemplative and mystical experience. Without a profound spiritual renewal in the church and in the pastoral ministry, a renewal which will manifest itself in both personal holiness and commitment to social justice, religion in our day will sink into the zone of comfort and shelter. The provision of opium for the people is not the purpose of the pastoral ministry.

Notes

CHAPTER 1
Spirituality and the Word of God

1   Paul Evdokimov, *L'Orthodoxie* (Neuchatel, Delachaux et Nestle, 1959), p. 113.
2   Charles Marson, *God's Cooperative Society* (Longmans, 1914), pp. 43, 51-2.
3   James Barr, *Fundamentalism* (SCM Press, 1978), p. 5.
4   E.R. Norman, *Christianity and the World Order* (Oxford University Press, 1979), pp. 76, 2.
5   Jim Wallis, *The Call to Conversion* (Lion Books, 1982), p. 28.
6   SCM Press (1961 edn).
7   Wes Seelinger, *Western Theology* (Atlanta, Forum House, 1973).
8   Oxford University Press, 1980.
9   Richard F. Lovelace, *Dynamics of Spiritual Life* (Paternoster Press, 1979), p. 218.
10 Martin Luther King, *Strength to Love* (Fontana, 1969), pp. 23-4. He speaks of 'creative maladjustment of a nonconforming minority' and says: 'Human salvation lies in the hands of the creatively maladjusted' (p. 24).
11 *Gaudium et Spes*, 9.
12 See J.L. Segundo, *The Liberation of Theology* (Maryknoll, Orbis, 1976), p. 9.

CHAPTER 2
Spirituality and Silence

1   Cited in Igumen Chariton of Valamo, *The Art of Prayer* (trans. E.D. Kadloubovsky and E.M. Palmer, Faber, 1966), p. 63.
2   Theological Orations, in *Christology of the Later Fathers* (ed. E.R. Hardy, Philadelphia, Westminster Press, 1954), p. 136.
3   Thomas à Kempis, *The Imitation of Christ*, 1.20.
4   Cited in George Woodcock, *Thomas Merton Monk and Poet* (Edinburgh, Canongate, 1978), pp. 41-2.

5 Roland Walls in *Solitude and Communion* (ed. A.M. Allchin, Oxford, SLG Press, 1977), p. 52.
6 Cited in Woodcock, op. cit., p. 77.
7 *The Cloud of Unknowing*, 6.83.
8 Martin Thornton, *Spiritual Direction* (SPCK, 1984).
9 Ibid. p. 19.
10 Martin Thornton, *English Spirituality* (SPCK, 1963), p. xiii.
11 Alasdair MacIntyre, *After Virtue* (Duckworth, 1981), p. 245.
12 Jean Daniélou, *The Lord of History* (Longmans, 1958), p. 77.
13 Nicholas Berdyaev, *Spirit and Reality* (Bles, 1939), p. 98.
14 'Choruses from the Rock' in *The Complete Poems and Plays of T.S. Eliot* (Faber, 1969), p. 149.
15 Henri J.M. Nouwen, *The Way of the Heart: Desert Spirituality and Contemporary Ministry* (Darton, Longman and Todd, 1981), p. 26.
16 Cited in Woodcock, op.cit., p. 153.

CHAPTER 3
Spirituality and Struggle

1 *Spiritual Direction*, op.cit., p. 14.
2 SPCK (1983).
3 Ibid., p. 71.
4 Ibid., p. 36.
5 Ibid., p. 88.
6 *The Book of Supreme Truth*, Ch. 4.
7 *The Adornment of the Spiritual Marriage*, Ch. 66.
8 *Conjectures of a Guilty Bystander* (1966), p. 58.
9 Darton, Longman and Todd (1980), p. 9.
10 Alastair V. Campbell, *Rediscovering Pastoral Care* (Darton, Longman and Todd, 1981), p. 26.
11 P.E.T. Widdrington in *The Return of Christendom* (Allen and Unwin, 1922), p. 102.
12 New York, Crossroads, 1981, p. 55.
13 *Otherworldliness and the New Testament* (SCM Press, 1955), p. 20.
14 Jim Wallis, op.cit., p. 34.
15 Sam Keen, *To A Dancing God* (Fontana, 1970), pp. 142ff.
16 Cited in *Walking on the Water: Women Talk about Spirituality* (ed. Sara Maitland and Jo Garcia, Virago Press, 1983), p. 7.
17 *Strength to Love*, op.cit., p. 62.
18 Cited in H.F.R. Catherwood, *The Christian in Industrial Society* (1964), pp. 28-9.
19 *Spirit and Reality*, op.cit., p. 98.

20 *Strength to Love*, op.cit., p. 15.
21 *Letters and Papers from Prison*, enlarged edn (Macmillan, 1972), p. 300.

CHAPTER 4
Spiritual Direction and the Contemporary Climate

1   Jean Leclercq, OSB, in *Fairacres Chronicle*, 12:3 (1979), p. 6.
2   This is stressed throughout the Eastern Christian tradition. See, for instance, the writings of the late Vladimir Lossky: for example, *The Mystical Theology of the Eastern Church* (James Clarke, 1957) and *Orthodox Theology: An Introduction* (New York, St Vladimir's Press, 1978).
3   Theodore Roszak, *Unfinished Animal* (Faber, 1977), p. 31.
4   E.R. Norman, op.cit., p. 84.
5   E.E. Larkin in *Theological Reflections on the Charismatic Renewal*, Proceedings of the Chicago Conference, 1-2 October 1976 (ed. John J. Haughey, SJ, Ann Arbor, Servant Books, 1978), p. 63.
6   On this matter see my book *The Social God* (Sheldon Press, 1981), Ch. 10, 'Is there a new religious fascism?' (pp. 97-115)
7   R.H. Tawney, *Religion and the Rise of Capitalism* (1926), p. 268.
8   *The Perception of Poverty in Europe* (Commission of European Communities, 1977).
9   Jim Wallis, *Agenda for Biblical People* (Harper and Row, 1976), p. 3.
10 *The Ladder of Divine Ascent* (ET, Harper, 1959), p. 203.

CHAPTER 5
Direction, Counselling and Psychotherapy

1   See R.A. Lambourne, 'Objections to a Proposed National Pastoral Organisation', *Contact* 35 (1971), pp. 25-7; Martin Thornton, *Spiritual Direction* op.cit., pp. 9-15.
2   See, for example, *The Politics of Experience* and *The Bird of Paradise* (Penguin, 1971 edn).
3   *English Spirituality*, op.cit., p. 11.
4   Lambourne, op.cit.
5   Roszak, op.cit., pp. 241-2.
6   Ibid., p. 242.
7   Irene Bloomfield in *Contact*, 61 (1978).
8   David Brandon, *Zen in the Art of Helping* (Routledge, 1976), pp. 32-3.

9   R.A. Lambourne in *Contact*, Spring 1974, p. 38.
10 Julian of Norwich, *Revelations of Divine Love*, Ch. 56.

CHAPTER 6
The Prophetic Dimension in Spiritual Direction

1   According to Canon John Tiller, *A Strategy for the Church's Ministry* (Church Information Office 1983) prophecy is difficult to combine with the priestly role because of the priest's relationship to the institution (p. 99).

2   *Theology* 82: 690 (November 1979), pp. 410–11.

3   J. Lindblom, *Prophecy in Ancient Israel* (1962), p. 121.

4   Roszak, op.cit., p. 60.

5   *Raids on the Unspeakable* (1966), p. 159.

6   Thomas Cullinan, OSB, in *The Eye of the Storm* (SCM Publications, n.d.), p. 15.

7   Oxford University Press (1980).

8   'Contemplation and Resistance', *Peace News*, 18 May 1973.

CHAPTER 7
Spiritual Direction and the Practice of Ministry

1   Martin Thornton, *English Spirituality*, op.cit., p. xiii.

2   Harper and Row (1980).

3   Schuller *et al.*, p. 4.

4   Ibid., p. 5.

5   Ibid., p. 74.

6   Ibid., p. 77.

7   Ibid., p. 244.

8   James Glasse, *Profession: Minister* (Abingdon Press, 1969).

9   Ian Ramsey, *Models and Mystery* (Oxford University Press, 1964), p. 61.

10 Henri J.M. Nouwen, *Creative Ministry* (Image Books, 1978), p. xxiii.

11 Urban T. Holmes, *The Future Shape of Ministry* (Seabury Press, 1971), Ch. 10.

12 Benedicta Ward, *Sayings of the Desert Fathers: the alphabetical collection* (Mowbrays, 1975), p. 88.

13 See David Wasdell, *Divide and Conquer: towards the multi-centre parish* (1974); *Let My People Grow* (1977); and many other publications, available from URCHIN, 115 Poplar High Street, London E14 0AE.

14   J.L. Segundo, *The Liberation of Theology* (Orbis, 1976), pp. 1, 185f.

CHAPTER 8
Brother Neville: Contemplative Among the Poor

1   Arthur Calder-Marshall, *No Earthly Command* (Rupert Hart Davies, 1957), p. 233: 'He was pitifully thin, though whether through illness or the practice of austerity I do not know. Nor do I know whether he was growing a beard or just had not shaved for some time. I had the impression that he did not know either. It was not his concern.'
2   See George Foulser, 'Cablestrasse', the *Observer*, 28 August 1960.
3   Ashley Smith, *The East Enders* (1961), p. 75.
4   Letter to Diognetus, 5–6.
5   See John Saward, *Perfect Fools* (Oxford University Press, 1980).
6   Theological Orations in *Christology of the Later Fathers* (ed. E.R. Hardy, Philadephia, Westminster Press, 1954), p. 136.
7   Jim Wallis, *Agenda for Biblical People*, op.cit., p. 3.

CHAPTER 9
Stanley Evans: The Kingdom of God in the Back Streets

1   *Junction* 14 (1961), p. 9.
2   Ibid. 11 (1960), p. 10.
3   *Towards Catholic Renewal: the Faith We Teach* (Jubilee Group and Church Literature Association 1977).
4   *Return to Reality: some essays on contemporary Christianity* (ed. S.G. Evans, Zeno Press, 1954), p. 10.
5   *Religion and the People*, January 1957.
6   For Widdrington see Maurice Reckitt, *P.E.T. Widdrington: a study in vocation and versatility* (SPCK, 1961). For a short account of Noel's theology see his *Jesus the Heretic* (Religious Book Club, 1940). For a general account of the tradition of social thought which they represented see John R. Orens, *Politics and the Kingdom: the legacy of the Anglican Left* (Jubilee Group, St Clement's House, Sirdar Road, London W11, 1981).
7   Stanley G. Evans, *The Church in the Back Streets* (Mowbrays, 1962) p. 48.
8   Stanley G. Evans, *In Evening Dress to Calvary* (SCM Press, 1965), p. 6.
9   Stanley G. Evans, *The Social Hope of the Christian Church* (Hodder and Stoughton, 1965), Ch. 10, pp. 245–56.

10 Ibid., p. 247ff on Arianism. For the influence of Noel see Noel's *Jesus the Heretic* op.cit., pp. 1-6 and *Socialism in Church History* (Frank Palmer, 1910), pp. 100-1.
11 *Junction*, 8 (October 1959).
12 *Le Milieu Divin* (1957), p. 88.
13 Conrad Noel, *Jesus the Heretic*, op.cit., p. 2.

CHAPTER 10
Hugh Maycock: Astonished at the Divine Beauty

1 From Hugh Maycock's notebooks, cited in A.M. Allchin *et al.*, *Francis Hugh Maycock: a tribute* (Oxford, S.G. Press, 1981), p. 2.
2 Ibid., p. 1.
3 The sermon is printed in *New Fire*, 3:20 (Autumn 1974), pp. 127-9.
4 Cited in Allchin, op.cit., p. 2.
5 *Retreats Today* (Association for Promoting Retreats, 1962), p. 83.
6 Rollo May, *Power and Innocence* (Souvenir Press, 1972), pp. 49-50.
7 F.H. Maycock, 'Edwin Muir and the Predicament of Man' in *Man Fallen and Free: Oxford essays on the condition of man* (ed. E.W. Kemp, Hodder and Stoughton, 1969), pp. 78-93. For the quotation see Muir's poem 'One Foot in Eden'.
8 D.H. Lawrence, 'Surgery for the Novel - or a bomb' in *Phoenix: the posthumous papers of D.H. Lawrence* (ed. Edward D. McDonald, Heinemann, 1961), p. 520.
9 Cited Allchin, op.cit., p. 4.
10 Ibid., pp. 4-5.
11 'The Dry Salvages' in *The Complete Poems and Plays of T.S. Eliot* (Faber, 1959), p. 190.

CHAPTER 11
Colin Winter: The Breaking Process

1 Colin Winter, *The Breaking Process* (SCM Press, 1981), p. 41.
2 Ibid., pp. 76-7.
3 Ibid., p. 5.
4 Ibid., pp. 37-8.
5 Charles Elliot, *Inflation and the Compromised Church* (Belfast, Christian Journals, 1975), p. 146.
6 Sam Keen, *To a Dancing God* (Fontana, 1970), pp. 141-60.
7 *Mystical Passion* (Paulist Press, 1977); *Earthy Mysticism: contemplation and the life of passionate presence* (New York, Crossroad, 1983).

8 *Mystical Passion*, op.cit., p. 4.
9 See, for example, *Beyond the Fragments* (Merlin, 1979), especially the essay by Sheila Rowbotham.
10 See E.R. Norman, op.cit. See also David Nicholls' comments in *Christianity Reinterpreted? a critical examination of the 1978 Reith Lectures* (ed. Kenneth Leech, Jubilee Group, 1982), pp. 8-16.
11 Henri J.M. Nouwen, *The Wounded Healer* (Doubleday, 1972).
12 Henri J.M. Nouwen, *Intimacy: pastoral psychological essays* (Notre Dame, Fides/Claretian, 1968), pp. 118-19.

CHAPTER 12
Spirituality and the Renewal of the Priesthood

1 Cf. R.J. Bocock, 'The Role of the Anglican Clergyman', *Social Compass*, 17:4 (1970), pp. 533-44.
2 Cited in L.W. Barnard, *C.B. Moss 1888-1964 Defender of the Faith* (Mowbrays, 1967).
3 Cf. James D. Glasse, op.cit.; J.L. Lowery, 'The Clergy, the Professional and Preparation for Ordained Ministry', *St Luke's Journal of Theology*, 14:4 (1971) and 15:1 (1972); J.H. Fichter, *Religion as an Occupation* (Notre Dame, 1961).
4 Urban T. Holmes, *The Future Shape of Ministry* (Seabury Press, 1971), Ch. 10.
5 Cf. Alastair V. Campbell, op.cit., p. 37.
6 Urban T. Holmes, *Ministry and Imagination* (Seabury Press, 1976), p. 7.
7 Martin Thornton, *Essays in Pastoral Reconstruction* (SPCK, 1960), pp. 86-7.
8 *Pastoral Theology: a reorientation* (SPCK, 1956), p. 14.
9 Monica Furlong, 'The Parson's Role Today', *New Christian*, 16 June 1966, p. 12.
10 Austin Farrar, *A Celebration of Faith* (1970), p. 110.
11 Thomas Merton, cited in George Woodcock, op. cit., p. 81.
12 *Ministerial Priesthood* (1968 edn), p. 260.
13 Cited in Woodstock, op.cit., p. 68.
14 See Aelred Cody, *A History of Old Testament Priesthood* (Rome, Pontifical Biblical Institute 1969, Analecta Biblica, 35).
15 In 2 Tim. 2.4 PG 62.612.
16 Ulrich Simon, *A Theology of Auschwitz* (Gollancz, 1967), p. 124.
17 Ibid., p. 127.
18 Herbert McCabe, 'Priesthood and Revolution', *Commonweal*, 20 September 1968, p. 626.

19   Urban T. Holmes, *The Priest in Community* (Seabury Press, 1978), p. 8.
20   Urban T. Holmes, *Ministry and Imagination*, op.cit., p. 5.
21   See Urban T. Holmes, *The Priest in Community*, op.cit., Ch. 4, 'The Priest as Angel' (pp. 96–121).
22   Eric Hayman, *Disciplines of the Spritual Life* (1957), p. 58.
23   *Rite or Ordination, Roman Rite* (Collegeville, Liturgical Press, 1970), p. 24.
24   Cited in Yves Congar in *Études de civilization medievale (IXe–XIIe siècles): melanges offerts à Edmond-Rene Labande* (Poitiers, 1973), p. 159.
25   Holmes, *The Priest in Community*, op.cit., p. 4.
26   Thornton, *Essays in Pastoral Reconstruction*, op.cit., p. 43.
27   Jurgen Moltmann, *The Church in the Power of the Spirit* (SCM Press, 1977), p. 24.

Acknowledgements

Acknowledgements are due to the following for permission to quote from the material listed:

Canongate Publishing Ltd, for an extract from *Thomas Merton, Monk and Poet* by George Woodcock.

Doubleday and Company, Inc., for an extract from *The Cloud of Unknowing* by William Johnston. Copyright © 1973 by William Johnston.

Faber and Faber Ltd, for extracts from 'Choruses from the "Rock"' and 'The Dry Salvages' from 'Four Quartets', all taken from *Collected Poems 1909-1962* by T.S. Eliot; and for extracts from *Unfinished Animal* by Theodore Roszak.

Harper and Row Publishers for extracts from *Ministry in America* by Dr David Schuller.

Oxford University Press, for an extract from *Christianity and the World Order* (1979) by E.R. Norman.

Routledge and Kegan Paul PLC, for an extract from *Zen in the Art of Helping* by David Brandon.

SCM Press Ltd, for an extract from *In Evening Dress to Calvary* by Stanley Evans; and for extracts from *The Breaking Process* by Colin Winter.

The Society for Promoting Christian Knowledge (SPCK), for an extract from *Liberating God* by Peter Selby.

Theology magazine, for an extract from an article by Richard Holloway.

A.P. Watt Ltd, on behalf of Miss D.E. Collins, for four lines from *The Flying Inn* by G.K. Chesterton.

Despite diligent enquiry, some copyright holders have proved impossible to trace, and to them the author and publisher extend their most sincere apologies.

145

Index

Antony, St   29
apophatic theology   18

Baker, Augustine   47
Barr, James   7
Basil, St   132
Baxter, Richard   48
Belton, F.G.   57
Berdyaev, Nicholas   28, 42
Bible,   see Word of God
Bloomfield, Irene   60-3
Body of Christ   9
Bonhoeffer, Dietrich   44
Brandon, David   63
Bucer, Martin   48
Bunyan, John   12

Cable Street   85-94
Calder-Marshall, Arthur   85
Campaign for Nuclear
  Disarmament   86, 96
Campbell, Alastair   35
Canterbury   105, 108
Caussade, J.P.de   108
charismatic movement   52
Charles de Foucauld   90
Chesterton, G.K.   101
Christa Seva Sangha   85
Christology   101
clericalism   127-8, 135-6

Clinical Theology   56
cloud   23
Coffin, William Sloane   7
Community of the
  Resurrection   85, 95
counselling   55-65
Cullinan, Thomas   71
Cyprian, St   132
Cyril of Jerusalem, St   132

Daily Worker   95
Dalston   96, 99
Daniélou, Jean   26
dark night   21-4, 60, 73
desert   21-2
Desert Fathers   19-22, 47, 66,
  70, 80
Diognetus   89
Dostoevsky, Fyodor   111

Ecclestone, Alan   34-5, 52
Eliot, T.S.   114
eucharist   110, 135
Eusebius   132
Evans, Stanley   95-104
Evdokimov, Paul   5

Farrer, Austin   130
formation   5-13
Fox, George   19-20

Freud, Sigmund   55
fundamentalism   7
Furlong, Monica   28, 130

Gandhi, Mohandas   30
Gaudium et Spes   14–15
Gilkey, Langdon   36f
gnosticism   8
Goon Show   17
Greenham Common   42f
Gregory of Nazianzus, St   19, 132
Gregory of Nyssa, St   132

Harton, F.P.   57
Hayman, Eric   134
hesychia   19, 71
Hesse, Hermann   111
Hippolytus   131
Holloway, Richard   67f
Holmes, Urban T.   79, 128, 133

Ignatius of Antioch, St   18
Ignatius Loyola, St   70
incarnation   38
innocence   42
intercession   134

John Chrysostom, St   132
John Climacus, St   54
John of the Cross, St   19, 23, 47, 52, 71, 73, 124
John the Solitary   19
Julian of Norwich   64
Jung, C.G.   55f

King, Martin Luther   12, 41, 42

Kingdom of God   9, 36–8, 98–9, 102, 136
Kyle, William   56

Laing, R.D.   56
Lake, Frank   56
Lambourne, Robert   56, 58
laughter   113
Lawrence, D.H.   112
Lovelace, Richard   12
Luther, Martin   12

McCabe, Herbert   133
Macarius of Egypt   132
MacIntyre, Alasdair   26
MacNamara, William   122–3
Marson, Charles   6–7
maturity   11–12
May, Rollo   110
Maycock, Hugh   105–114, 121–2, 124
Merton, Thomas   20, 30, 33f, 43, 52, 69, 71–2, 130–1
Moberly, R.C.   130
Muir, Edwin   106, 111–2

Namibia   115–7, 119
National Front   39
Nazism   38
Neville, Brother   85–94, 121–2, 124
Noel, Conrad   99
Norman, E.R.   124
Notting Dale   117
Nouwen, Henri   29, 79, 125

Origen   131

Palmer, Neville   see Neville

Paul, St   9–13
poverty   53
priesthood   127–136
progress   9–11
prophecy   43f, 66–74, 135
psychotherapy   55–65

Ramsey, Ian   78
revolution   133
Robinson, John A.T.   9, 106
Roszak, Theodore   59–60, 68
Ruysbroeck, John van   33, 73

Saward, John   12, 72
Schuller, David   75–7
Scripture   see Word of God
Seeliger, Wes   9
Segundo, J.L.   15, 80
Selby, Peter   31
silence   17–30
Simon, Ulrich   132
spiritual direction   24–5, 47–81

Symeon, St   19

Tawney, R.H.   41, 53
Temple, William   50
Tertullian   131
Theophan the Recluse   19
Thomas à Kempis   19
Thornton, Martin   25, 31, 57,
   75, 129, 135
Tractarians   47

Wallis, Jim   8–9, 37f
Ward, Reginald Somerset   57,
   112
Wasdell, David   80
Weil, Simone   39, 52
Westminster Pastoral
   Foundation   56
Widdrington, P.E.T.   56
Wilder, Amos   37
Winter, Colin   52, 115–126
Word of God   5–16